Story of Char's Brother

THANK YOU!
for your part in our lives and
the lives of many others.

2ω

D0757536

DON'T CALL ME POOR

A Mother Grieves and Grows as her
Teenage Son Courageously Fights Cancer

EVADENE STRANSKE

Order this book online at www.trafford.com
or email orders@trafford.com

Most Trafford titles are also available at major online book retailers.

Front cover photo taken 1/20/1971 by staff photographer Mel Scheiltz of the *Rocky
Mountain News* owned by Scripps Media, Inc. Used by permission.

Scripture passages quoted throughout this book are taken from the King James Version unless otherwise noted.

Scripture quotations marked (NIV) are taken from the Holy Bible, New International Version®,
NIV®. Copyright © 1973, 1978, 1984, 2011 by Biblica, Inc.™ Used by permission of Zondervan.
All rights reserved worldwide. www.zondervan.com The "NIV" and "New International Version"
are trademarks registered in the United States Patent and Trademark Office by Biblica, Inc.™

Printed in the United States of America.

ISBN: 978-1-4669-4176-2 (sc)
ISBN: 978-1-4669-4177-9 (hc)
ISBN: 978-1-4669-4175-5 (e)

Library of Congress Control Number: 2012910165

Trafford rev. 08/08/2012

 www.trafford.com

North America & international
toll-free: 1 888 232 4444 (USA & Canada)
phone: 250 383 6864 ♦ fax: 812 355 4082

For

The Committed Children
God Entrusted to Us

Charlotte Holcomb, Ray, Tim
Faith Hintz, Susan Carlson

and

Our Sixteen Wonderful Grandchildren

Jeanette (Cook), Dan, Doug, Phil Holcomb
Jon, Clarissa (Fugazzotto) Stranske
Tim, Gail (Hampsmire), Sarah Stranske
Tom, Steve, Marissa, Andrew, Christopher Hintz
Josiah, David Carlson

and

Our Miracle Great Grandchildren

Annika, Zachariah, Shereena, Ezekiel, Daniel Cook
Talia Holcomb
Micah, Lucy Holcomb
Maiya Holcomb

Contents

Preface

God challenged our lives, and the life of each member of our family, through the incredible events surrounding the life-struggle of our son, Darryl, as he was diagnosed with cancer. As we have periodically shared the battles, the lessons learned, and the stimulating challenge to a vast number of people through his lengthy illness, we have repeatedly been encouraged to write his story for others to read. Remembering many difficult lessons learned and God's gracious dealing with her—and with our whole family—during this heart-breaking time, Evadene felt compelled to share her story—Darryl's story, our family's story—believing that it might help and encourage others who struggle in similar circumstances. We also felt that this story needed to be written to provide our own family a record that would assist us in remembering how God worked in all of our lives through the difficult months of Darryl's illness.

Fortunately, she did not have to reconstruct this story from memory. Whether out of the country or in some other setting that removed us from other family members, she has always done an exceptional job of communicating, in detail, the things that were going on in our lives. Her Mother in particular, but also some of our children and other family members, carefully preserved the numerous letters that Evadene wrote throughout the years. These letters, dozens of them, were later returned to her. She saved all of them, along with the hundreds of letters received from all over the country, and even the world, as the media and individuals joined in sharing Darryl's story. That has provided a full and accurate source of information for her as she began to carefully record the history of this committed son, Darryl, along with the impact that his life has had on our family and others far beyond our family circle.

As I have had the privilege of assisting Evadene by doing some of the editing work on this overview of Darryl's life, I have been challenged anew by the commitment of this son that God brought into our family. Darryl began life as a strong-willed youngster and was certainly not perfect, but he provides an example of what God can and will do with a life that is yielded to Him. God saw fit to allow Darryl to suffer but, also, to triumph greatly in that suffering. And in that process God used him to eternally challenge each one in our family, as well as a vast host of other people.

Evadene is especially grateful to our daughter Susan for hours spent in final preparation of this manuscript for publication. Without her help, it may not have reached completion.

May this record of Darryl's victorious response to suffering energize many others to make a whole-hearted commitment to our great and loving God. It is our prayer that, as God has been glorified through Darryl, He may be glorified in each of our lives as we serve Him during the continuing days that He gives us on this earth.

We pray, too, that Evadene's honest sharing of her feelings, her struggles, and the impact of all of this on our family along with the way in which God met our needs during these difficult years will be a help and an encouragement to many others as they read this account.

Harvey Stranske

Chapter 1

THE YEAR WE BURNED THE CANDLE

Colorful wax trickled down the knobby sides of the candle in our dimly lit dining room. That previously unlit white Christmas tree candle with embedded multicolored balls had been our Christmas dinner table centerpiece for several years but, for this occasion, I decided to light it. Something compelled me to change tradition by striking a match to our treasured possession.

Today we celebrated. It was Christmas Eve—the day our family traditionally remembered Christmas. But more importantly, Darryl, our thirteen-year-old son had been released from the hospital. After six months of examining and probing, doctors felt confident that they had finally discovered the reason for the periodic pain in his neck. They removed his sub-maxillary salivary gland, generating hope for Darryl's full recovery. No doubt, he would soon be back to his usual energetic self. With relief, we brought Darryl home from the hospital the morning of December 24. He had a huge bandage on his neck covering the incision from surgery completed three days earlier. Although he couldn't move his head very fast, he appeared to be on the mend.

Darryl had purchased Christmas gifts early with money earned on his paper route. In spite of his long illness and time spent in the hospital, he was ready. His evident eagerness rippled through the family as we enjoyed this rare occasion of having our whole family together. Charlotte, Ray and

Tim, our older children, had driven home from Biola College in California; Darryl's younger sisters, Faith and Susan, were on vacation from elementary school. Following family tradition, we sat down to an elegant Christmas Eve dinner, each one wearing something red or green to make the occasion more festive. I put the ornate Christmas candle in its usual place, but this year we watched the candle burn as we ate our meal. As the flame reached the first colored balls, streams of mixed colors slithered down the tree, unlocking the beauty hidden inside.

Family photo by our Christmas Tree 1970.
Back row: Charlotte, Evadene, Harvey, Susan, Ray, Tim (holding Snowball);
Front row: Faith, Darryl

We chatted, sharing experiences of recent months—our conversation enhanced by the beauty of that changing candle producing a striking display before us. After dinner, everyone joined in the clean-up process before gathering around our fragrant Christmas tree. Before any gifts were opened, we made it a practice to remember the real reason for the season by reading

Luke 2—that awesome story about the birth of Jesus; and we took time to thank God for His great gift.

Darryl entered into this time of remembrance with reverence, but when we completed reading we again noted his exuberance. He couldn't wait. He didn't care about what he might receive. He eagerly looked forward to sharing the things he had lovingly purchased to give. He gave his youngest sister, Susan, a toy Easy Bake oven that really baked small cakes and brownies. Faith, four years older than Susan, received a tiny toy sewing machine that actually sewed. Together with his older brother Ray, Darryl gave Dad a power keyhole saw. I received a lovely lace tablecloth.

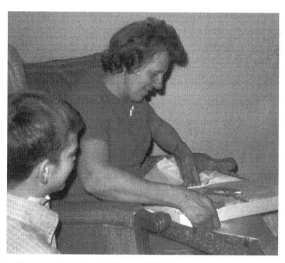

Darryl looks on as I open the lace tablecloth he had purchased for me

To watch Darryl's elation as each of us opened his gifts gave me a feeling of intense fulfillment. What a privilege to see a child mature from the "gimme" stage to the "I want to give you" stage. "He is going to be some man when he grows up," I mused quietly to myself.

Christmas Day brought more joyous merriment. We shared a scrumptious turkey dinner, savoring animated conversation after months of separation. What precious time we shared together. But, as the week continued, dark clouds broke into our lives. Darryl approached me one

3

evening to reveal red blotches erupting on his body. He then added that many of his glands seemed to be swollen. "Whatever could this new turn of events mean," I wondered.

I quickly called Dr. Dragel, the surgeon who had operated on Darryl. I explained Darryl's symptoms and he told me to contact our family doctor. I made an appointment with Dr. Kurtz for late afternoon on the following day. Our older children planned to leave for California after lunch that day and I didn't want to miss any time with them.

The morning bustled with activity as three college kids prepared to leave. Ray even put some finishing touches on a term paper due on the day he returned to school. Since they planned to depart around one o'clock, we traded our usual evening dinner with a big meal at noon to provide an added boost for their travels. I wanted them to leave with full stomachs since I often felt concerned about their eating; college expenses kept them on a tight budget. As they prepared to leave after dinner, the boys discovered a car problem. They had to make repairs before they could go and were still working on the car when I took Darryl to the doctor at 3:30. Since they intended to be gone when we returned, we said our "good byes" as Darryl and I left.

Dr. Kurtz greeted me and then took Darryl into the examining room alone. As the minutes ticked on, growing concern gripped me. What's taking so long? What's wrong? Finally, Darryl returned and Dr. Kurtz asked to talk to me alone. My fears rapidly increased and seemed to confirm my suspicions. There must be something drastically wrong. Offering me a chair, Dr. Kurtz with whom we had a trusting relationship, looked into my face and then to the floor as if to gain time for what he had to tell me. At last, he shared what he had found.

"Mrs. Stranske," he began, pausing, "I examined Darryl with great care. I found that he is abnormally large for his age and the point of development he is at sexually. I am quite sure that he has some type of lymphoma. Because of the New Years holiday followed by the weekend, it would do no good to put him in the hospital now. Nothing in the way of diagnostic testing is done in the hospital over a weekend like this. So we will admit him to Porter Hospital on Monday morning to verify what is happening. I hope that tests will prove me wrong, but I don't think they will. At this point, please don't tell Darryl what I have told you. We want to have a definitive diagnosis first."

Thoughts crashed through my mind a million miles a minute. Lymphoma! Since medical things have always interested me, I knew what that meant. Lymphoma is cancer of the lymph system. Why did this shocking news have to break into the end of this idyllic Christmas? Why did such a horrible sentence have to enter into our lives at all—ever! Maybe Dr. Kurtz was wrong. Hadn't he suggested this only as a possibility? Maybe, just maybe, he was mistaken. Maybe, it only looked like lymphoma. Even that ray of hope didn't remove the lump from my throat or take away the feeling that I'd been hit with a ton of bricks.

"Thank you, Dr. Kurtz," I said and walked into the waiting room where Darryl sat looking at a magazine. "Okay Honey, let's go," I said as I started toward the car. Our appointment had been late and darkness descends early on Denver in December. Thankful for that early darkness, I felt it might help me hide my feelings from Darryl.

He waited until we were in the car and driving home before Darryl questioned, "Mom, why did Dr. Kurtz want to talk to you alone?"

Now my thoughts began racing again. "Why hadn't I anticipated this question?" I scolded myself. We had always been open and above-board in our family, so how could I answer such a question when the doctor had given specific instructions that I shouldn't tell Darryl what he had told me? Guardedly I replied, "Well Darryl, he just wanted to talk to me about your physical condition."

"What did he say?" Darryl pumped.

"He said that he is not sure what is wrong, but he wants to put you in the hospital again on Monday for more tests."

"But why couldn't I be there? It was about me," Darryl prodded, increasing the pressure.

"Darryl," I replied, "Sometimes a doctor wants to talk to a mother alone. This was one of those times, so let's leave it at that." Darryl remained very quiet the rest of the way home. With his sharp mind working overtime, he recognized that something was radically wrong.

To my total surprise, I found our college kids still at home when we arrived. The boys had finally worked through the problem with the car and scrambled to finish their repairs as we drove into the driveway. This half-day delay put added pressure on them to leave quickly in order to get back to California in time to resume responsibilities at school.

I pulled Charlotte into the bedroom with me as soon as we got into the house and told her what Dr. Kurtz had said. A look of deep pain spread across her face. As a graduate nurse, she understood the implications of lymphoma. Without hesitation she made her way into the garage to share the sad news with her brothers. I drew my husband, Harvey, aside and shared the negative report with him. We couldn't cry. We had to keep up a front before Darryl and the two younger girls. Each of us found it difficult to dam up those feelings and pretend that everything was fine. Both our smiles and our conversation became wooden.

We had soup for a quick supper. This pleased me since I didn't feel up to making or eating our normal dinner meal. My stomach felt full of rocks. The hot soup soothed my aching mind and body.

Before we left the table, we did something we had not done before. It seemed so appropriate right then. We joined hands and together sang the old hymn, *Blest Be the Tie that Binds*:

> Blest be the tie that binds
> Our hearts in Christian love!
> The fellowship of kindred minds
> Is like to that above.

Before our Father's throne
We pour our ardent prayers;
Our fears, our hope, our aims are one,
Our comforts and our cares.

We share our mutual woes,
Our mutual burdens bear;
And often for each other flows
The sympathizing tear.

When we asunder part
It gives us inward pain;
But we shall still be joined in heart,
And hope to meet again.

The pathos of that moment left us with deep emotional feelings; tears trickled down our faces. That experience remains etched on my mind as if inscribed with indelible ink. After singing those words a settled peace came over me. I reflected on the closeness of our family and the inner strength that brought. Beyond the support drawn from a loving family, that peace involved more than human relationships. Our Father in Heaven had taken care of us in the past, and I knew we could trust Him now. As the song instructs, we needed to pour out our prayers before our Father's throne and believe God's promises to us. We needed to rest on those eternal truths.

My thoughts flashed back to our Christmas Eve dinner. I pondered my decision to burn the candle.

Char observes the beauty created by the flame in our Christmas Tree Candle

The inner beauty of our candle had not been visible apart from the destructive flame. Was there some special meaning in this? Was this an omen of coming events? Was Darryl's life going to melt away in the same way the candle had begun to dissolve? Would I have the privilege of seeing this fine son grow to manhood as I had anticipated a few short days ago? Then I thought of that momentous time when Darryl came into this world. God gave Darryl to us as a special gift. He had answered prayer and worked miraculous healing in my body that allowed Darryl to come into being. Wouldn't He preserve the gift He had given to us?

Chapter 2

IT'S A BOY

"Oh, it's so good to hear a baby cry! You say it's a boy? That's just what I wanted," I said as everyone in the delivery room scurried around to take care of this newborn and his mother. I already had three beautiful children, ages seven, eight and nine—two of whom were boys. But the cry of this newborn boy was an unexpected miracle.

We were missionaries in Africa and two years earlier I had given birth to another baby—a tiny little boy—in Khartoum, the capital of the Sudan. During that pregnancy, I had a severe case of toxemia and the doctor had ordered a huge dose of morphine the evening before I delivered to keep me from going into eclampsia. That medication sealed the fate of our baby. The doctor explained that he had not expected him to be born alive anyhow. My illness had kept nourishment from getting to his little body to enable him to grow. Baby Donny only lived for six hours. The hospital staff had little knowledge of how to care for a 3½-pound baby. The hospital had no incubator and no oxygen.

I failed to respond in normal fashion after the baby's birth. My kidneys continued to malfunction. In most cases toxic conditions subside after the baby is born but my problems persisted. Completing an examination, the doctor informed me that my illness had damaged my kidneys beyond repair. He then added the ominous words that I should never plan to have another child. His devastating pronouncement made my grieving for the tiny baby that I had lost even more heart-wrenching.

Circumstances surrounding this excruciating period added to my despair and prevented vital healing. For some months before the baby's delivery, Harvey and I had temporarily resided in Khartoum to enable Harvey to work on Arabic language projects. Two months before my due date, we left Khartoum to travel to Doro in the southern Sudan. We planned to arrive just in time to meet our two oldest children, Char and Ray (ages seven and six) who were returning from boarding school in Addis Ababa, Ethiopia; they had been away from home for nine months. MAF (Missionary Aviation Fellowship) would fly them to Doro, the closest airstrip to our home in Wadega. We would then drive the remaining forty-two miles to Wadega.

It took three days to make the four-hundred-mile trip from Khartoum to Doro, a grueling journey under the best of circumstances. Being pregnant and not feeling well made the trip even more difficult. I had noticed that my legs were swollen before we left Khartoum but had not asked a doctor about it. I reasoned that the doctor who would deliver our baby lived in Doro, and I would see him when we picked up our children.

Arriving in Doro, we watched with delight as the small MAF plane descended, bringing back Char and Ray. In the excitement of reuniting with them and the hubbub of getting ready to go on to Wadega, I almost forgot about the problem with my swollen legs. At the last minute I asked our mission doctor, Reuben Balzer, about it. A quick exam changed all of our plans. He discovered albumin in my urine and that my blood pressure was out of control.

Dr. Balzer told me that it would be unsafe to travel and ordered me to bed. Spending more than a month in bed in Doro did not improve my toxemia. As the time approached, Dr. Balzer decided that he couldn't take responsibility for delivering our baby. He did not have necessary equipment to meet anticipated emergency needs, so he ordered me flown back to Khartoum to be cared for in the British government hospital.

MAF flew our family back to Khartoum and I was taken directly to the hospital. Our little Donny began his brief stay on earth the following morning. It seemed that I started on the road to recovery but then, because of decisions made for our family, my health deteriorated.

Less than a week after my discharge from the hospital, our mission leaders decided that Harvey needed to be at our annual field conference back in the remote region of Doro. The agenda included evaluating the use of Sudanese Colloquial Arabic in tribal ministries. Harvey had studied Colloquial Arabic extensively and had begun to translate the Gospel of John, a project that would benefit all missions working in the southern Sudan. He was also experimenting with the possible use of Arabic script in writing tribal languages. With that background, mission leadership felt it necessary for him to participate in these vital discussions. I was neither strong enough to travel nor sufficiently recovered to risk being in a secluded mission station without emergency medical facilities. Therefore, I would need to stay in Khartoum with our three children.

I was still not well enough to care for our children. Fellow missionaries assured both Harvey and me that they would watch them while he was away. Our friends meant well and tried to care for our children but they were all busy with a multitude of other responsibilities. They didn't need or have time for the extra burden of three active, young children. Harvey's departure was difficult for our children. Charlotte and Ray were currently "home" for three months of treasured vacation from boarding school but because of my illness, they never reached our home during that break. Instead, we needed to stay at the mission station near medical help for my sake.

This certainly wasn't the vacation that two homesick kids had been anticipating. All the disruption did not make them the most cooperative children in the world either. Looking out from my bed through the curtained window I saw those three precious children walk by with uncombed hair and unhappy faces, and my heart cried out, "Whatever is going to happen to those kids?" How I longed for needed strength to care for them. I struggled physically and emotionally in my weakened condition as my distraught mind grappled with more than I could handle.

That night I turned off the light and tried to sleep. As I closed my eyes a strange, ethereal sensation descended over me. I felt myself sinking into a sea of water—sinking, sinking, sinking,—until nearly submerged. I had to turn on the light and stare at it to get any release. Again and again, as I closed my eyes and tried to sleep, that sensation overwhelmed me. Only by opening my eyes and gazing at the light could I free myself from the illusion of disappearing into the depths. Deep darkness seemed to envelop me.

Beth Wordie, the Australian nurse who was staying in the room to help meet my needs, was away for a bit but when she returned to the room I told her, "Beth, I'm sorry but I just have to have that light on. I feel like I'm sinking, but when I look at the light I feel like I can keep afloat. When I don't look at the light I sense that I'm drowning. It's only by looking at the light that I keep myself from going under. I don't know what's the matter, but that's how I feel."

"It's all right, Evadene. We'll just leave the light on," she replied.

I continued to struggle far into the night, watching the light, and then slipping into troubled sleep. Jarred to wakefulness, I would again experience that sinking feeling. Dear Beth. She kept watching me; encouraging me. At last, around 2 AM, I dropped off into a restful sleep and Beth turned off the light.

After a doctor examined me the next day, he told Beth that he didn't think I would make it. Suddenly, the episode of the previous night took on new meaning as it became apparent to her that I had been fighting for my very life.

Wanting to do what would be best for me, our missionary friends decided to move me to our language school home in Omdurman, the city across the Nile River from Khartoum. They felt that removing me from close proximity to the children would be beneficial. That day "happened" to be the monthly day of prayer for our mission and its work that extended across the wide part of the continent of Africa. As our missionary family in the Khartoum area prayed that day, they united in pleading with God to spare my life.

The next day Harvey returned by plane from the Southern Sudan greeted by the stunning news, "We're sorry, but Evadene got worse after you left. The doctor doesn't think she will live. We took her over to Omdurman as we thought that it would be quieter for her there."

"Oh no! How could that have happened? She seemed to be doing so well!" Not waiting for the little MAF plane to get unloaded, Harvey asked friends to take him to Omdurman as quickly as possible. The six miles or so, which separated the airport from our language school, seemed to stretch on forever. He was thankful that the drawbridge over the Nile River was not open to allow an Arab dhow to pass through, an expected hindrance at that time of day.

Arriving at the language school, he banged on the huge metal gate. One of the houseboys opened the gate and Harvey rushed into the mission compound—an area surrounded by seven to eight-foot-high mud walls. A labyrinth of such mud-walled enclosures covers all of Omdurman. Greeted by one of the missionary women who lived and worked at the language school, he demanded, "Where's Evadene? How is she?"

"Evadene is in the back bedroom. So sorry we don't have a phone over here so we could let people in Khartoum know that she is much better today. From the time of their prayer meeting yesterday her situation turned around. It's obvious that God touched her as God's people were praying."

From inside the room, I heard Harvey talking out on the verandah. I rushed out of the room and threw my arms around his neck for a much-needed embrace. "You'll never know how good it is to have you back," I cried. "Can't I go back to Khartoum with you?" After packing up my things, we headed back.

God had touched my body and brought me back from the brink of death, yet He had not provided total healing. I continued to struggle and questioned why God didn't complete the healing process that He had begun. Harvey and I reminded ourselves that God is sovereign and, in His overwhelming love, He always does what is right and good for us. Beyond that, what He does in the lives of His children will also bring glory to Him. Even though I knew these truths and joined in affirming that I believed them, the distressing word of my doctor indicating that I should never again plan to have children kept ringing in my ears. For me, the anguish of that thought was near unbearable.

To provide for further recuperation and give us family time with our two children who would soon return to school, we spent the following month in a missionary vacation facility in Asmara, Eritrea. Char and Ray found it hard to return to Addis Ababa from Asmara without ever getting "home" for vacation. Although we understood their disappointment, my health prevented us from fulfilling their desire to spend time at our remote mission station home. After sending them off to school, we completed our time in Asmara and returned to Khartoum.

In spite of my continuing physical and emotional problems, we made the decision to return to our isolated mission station—our home in Wadega. I tried to make a go of it, but my struggles only increased. The following months produced no noticeable change in my kidney function. It became apparent that it was not wise for me to remain in our remote location. Mission leadership concurred that we should leave our bush station and go back to Khartoum.

We were thankful for the caring ministry of a CMS (Church Missionary Society) doctor during our time in Omdurman and Khartoum. As she worked with me, it became clear to her and to us that I would not regain my health in Africa. My physical condition necessitated a return to the United States for further medical assistance. Mission leadership agreed even though we lacked one year of fulfilling our normal four-year term. With the decision finalized, we arranged for Charlotte and Ray to leave school a month early. They flew into Khartoum and we left for New York.

In New York, each of us endured the extensive physical exams required when we returned for home assignment. As our consulting mission doctor, Dr. Frame, reviewed my recent history, he shook his head and said, "Lady, I don't know why you are here. You were at death's door for 3 ½ months. I really don't know why you are still alive."

While in New York I noticed that Charlotte had a deep cough and almost jokingly told Harvey, "That cough sounds awful! I hope she doesn't have TB or something."

"Oh, she'll no doubt be okay after we're home for awhile," he responded. For the moment, we forgot our interchange in the excitement of flying on to California.

After visiting Harvey's parents in Southern California for a week, we traveled north to Turlock, my family's home area. We planned to spend our year of home assignment there. As we left southern California, we just missed a letter addressed to us. Harvey's parents forwarded it on to Turlock. By the time we received it, three weeks had elapsed since we left New York. The letter informed us that Charlotte's chest x-rays, taken during her physical in New York, looked suspicious. It instructed us to get her to a qualified doctor without delay. We made an appointment to see Dr. Everett Johnson, the TB specialist for Stanislaus County. He phoned a few days after our appointment to inform us that Charlotte did, indeed, have tuberculosis. In fact, she had a cavity on one side and lesions on the other. It appeared that she could lose one lung. What a shock to discover that my half-jesting words in New York had taken on new significance.

Dr. Johnson warned us that since one of Charlotte's lungs had been so overwhelmed by the disease, we would need to be very careful with her. She must get to bed early each evening and we must take every precaution to keep her from getting flu or pneumonia. Reemphasizing the gravity of her situation, he told us that if she got one of these illnesses he could do nothing for her. She would die. Overcome by the impact of what he told me, I couldn't help but wonder what would have happened to Charlotte had my illness not forced us to return to the U.S. a year early.

After 2 ½ years of treatment, Dr. Johnson considered Charlotte well enough to return to Africa. Filled with gratitude, we recognized that Charlotte's recovery became possible because God brought us home at a critical time in the development of this life-threatening disease. In spite of my questioning struggles about my incomplete healing in Africa, it was obvious that God had not forgotten to care for us or listen to us when our mission family prayed for my healing. He always works for our ultimate good.

During our time in America, God spoke to my heart through a very special book. *Crowded to Christ*, by L. E. Maxwell, profoundly affected me. As I began to lay hold of and follow principles taught, God brought healing to my mind and body. Speaking of Romans 8:28 (KJV), "And we know that all things work together for good to them that love God...," Maxwell quotes George Mueller:

> In 1,000 things it is not 999 of them which work together for good, but 999 plus one .... Can we thank God for the thing which is, to every appearance, against us? What is our "plus one?"[1]

> Begin then to obey the command, "*In every thing give thanks.*" More practical still, begin "giving thanks *always* for all things." Without even wishing for a change of circumstances, begin to thank God for the trial, the sickness, the insult.[2]

Gripped by these truths, I realized that I even needed to thank God for taking our tiny baby, and for my illness, and for everything that God allowed in my life, even though I might never understand or see any reason for them

---

[1] L. E. Maxwell, *Crowded to Christ* (Grand Rapids: Wm. B. Eerdmans Publishing Company, 1952), page 94.

[2] Ibid., page 95

from my human perspective. As I obeyed and thanked God for these trials, I began to experience God's full and complete healing.

During Charlotte's prolonged treatment, I also saw Dr. Johnson for further evaluation of my condition. He gave me an extensive and very thorough physical after which he informed me that he could find no continuing trace of any kidney problem. Since my kidneys were now functioning, I could plan to have another child!

After over a year of struggle and trying to come to grips with the medical rationale that I should not have any more children, God had granted full healing to me and blessed us with a new little life. This fact generated my exuberant reaction when I heard the lusty cry of my new baby boy. The tiny one we lost in Africa was never strong enough to cry, so when God's precious replacement gift let out a loud cry it was music to my ears and produced my sentiment, "Oh, it's so good to hear a baby cry!" Since the baby that died in Africa had been a boy, I was ecstatic when I heard that I had a son. With deep gratitude, I embraced Darryl Stanley, this strong, 8 pound, 3 ounce, special treasure in my arms. God not only performed a miracle of completely healing my body, He also completed my emotional healing with this cherished gift.

It didn't take long to realize that our new son had a very strong personality. He demonstrated this in a forceful manner on his first birthday. For some time, I had nursed him only once a day in the early morning before I got up; now I decided to wean him. Changing the known routine on this special day in his life, I picked Darryl up from his crib and began to move toward placing him in his high chair in the kitchen. Before I got to the kitchen he began protesting with vigor, pounding me on my chest with his little fists, and crying all the way into the kitchen.

Yes, challenging days lay ahead, but as Darryl continued to grow, he became an active child with an engaging personality and a winsome smile. With his brown hair and the prettiest dark brown eyes that I had ever seen, he brought special joy into my life, our home, and to our whole family.

Chapter 3

SNAPSHOTS OF DARRYL'S
PRESCHOOL YEARS IN AFRICA

From his earliest years Darryl lived an extraordinary life. At fifteen months, he returned with us to the Sudan to a remote, undeveloped mission station.

The Sudanese government refused to allow our mission to build a permanent house of brick. Instead, they gave permission to frame a structure out of slotted angle iron. The walls and roof were then covered with corrugated aluminum roofing. The completed building looked like something constructed out of a giant erector set. We had no ceiling, so we laid ten foot pieces of angle iron across the base of our A-frames to create a place to tie essential mosquito nets. Those nets provided protection, enabling us to sleep at night.

Riwoto house

One day, after living in Riwoto for about six months, I sat in a chair in our living room and wrote letters. As often happened, strong winds buffeted our erector set house. Suddenly, an exceptional gust shook the whole house. I heard a loud bang and Darryl began to cry. That gust of wind dislodged one of the ten foot pieces of slotted angle iron laying across the base of the A-frames for our mosquito nets. Although Darryl played at my feet, I didn't see that ten foot piece of iron fall onto our little son's back. It happened so fast!

I looked in horror at a gaping slash in Darryl's back, open from below his right shoulder across to the left side of his back, exposing his ribs. The nearest doctor resided at Logotok mission station one hundred miles away. We had no 9-1-1 number to call—we didn't even have a phone. We sat alone in a wilderness corner of the Sudan.

"Harvey," I shouted, "Darryl is hurt! He's hurt bad! What should we do?"

Looking at that shocking sight, Harvey responded, "I guess the only thing we can do is try to get him to Logotok. I hope he can last that long." With little more than a pause, Harvey continued, "There isn't enough gas in the truck; I'll go out and gas it up [he had to siphon gas from 50 gallon barrels which we hauled 120 miles from the nearest gas pump to our isolated station]. You try to get some clothes together. We may have to be there a few days." It took close to an hour for Harvey to get the truck gassed up and ready to go.

Meanwhile, I struggled to gather my wits about me. I tried to put tape across Darryl's cavernous wound to close it, but bleeding kept the tape from sticking. I then covered the massive injury with some sheet bandages and gave him some salt water for shock and a small phenobarbital pill. Thankful now that his wounds were not bleeding profusely, I walked around holding him in my arms endeavoring to comfort him. At the same time, I prepared for our trip by directing the Taposa young man who worked for us: "Get that tin trunk and put it here. Now get the clothes out of that box [we didn't have any chest of drawers yet] and put them in the trunk. Put that dress and those trousers in the trunk." In that rather unorthodox way, we gathered necessary items for our long trip to the doctor.

On a normal day, that trip of one hundred miles to Logotok took four hours because of the rough dirt roads filled with potholes. When we hit some of those potholes, I often bounced so high that my head hit the roof— usually I also protectively held a little one tightly on my lap. Accumulation of rigorous bouncing had created a pronounced indentation in the cab ceiling above my seat where my head had repeatedly hit; we did not have seat belts. We crossed many stream beds, never knowing if they would be filled with water. Irish bridges (paved roadways over huge concrete pipes to allow a stream of water to flow under the road) provided enhanced crossings over many streams. Heavy rains in the mountains south of the road, however, often made these helpful crossings impassable. This didn't happen often, but sometimes we had to stop for several hours until the water subsided. We knew that twenty-two of these Irish Bridges lay between Riwoto and Logotok in addition to twelve regular bridges.

Waiting to cross a stream at a time when the water was running high

Grateful that streams ran low on this day, we flew over the bumps faster than usual. Darryl lay across my lap with his legs stretched out across the rest of the seat. Quieted by Phenobarbital, he slept part of the way. We hoped and prayed that he would live long enough to get to the doctor. We made that "four-hour trip" in just three hours, but had already lived through four agonizing hours after the accident had opened his little back.

We had a short-wave radio at Riwoto, and we talked with each of our other Sudan stations every morning at a scheduled time. We appreciated that radio so much as it reduced our feeling of isolation. When planning to travel to one of our sister mission stations over those vast stretches of isolated road, we shared travel plans, including expected times of departure from our home and arrival time at our destination. However, we had not planned our travel that day so had not informed our friends of our trip. After signing off in the morning, we had no way of contacting fellow workers unless we had prearranged an additional time to talk. Therefore, Dr. Doug Reitsma and his wife, Kim, greeted us with surprise as we drove up. As Doug walked to the car, I said, "We have a badly hurt little boy here. We need some help."

Pulling back some of the covering over Darryl's back, our special doctor friend responded, "Yes, I guess you do. Let's get him into the clinic and try to sew that up."

I stayed with Dr. Reitsma and Kim as they anesthetized Darryl. Then, with exceptional gentleness, they closed that little laid-open back with twenty stitches. Darryl had sustained a major injury for a little tyke only twenty-two months of age. Dr. Doug marveled that that ten-foot length of angle iron had opened Darryl's entire back, yet had missed tendons, muscles, and bones, and had not injured any vital organ. We rejoiced that our little boy survived and that, in a miraculous way, God had spared him from injury that could have crippled him for life.

We appreciated Dr. Reitsma a great deal and believed that God had provided the best possible medical assistance for us missionaries in the southern Sudan. Dr. Reitsma had planned to be away on vacation at this time but he had become ill with malaria. This caused their family to delay their vacation for a week. Once again, we saw the hand of our sovereign God who kept our doctor home to meet Darryl's great need. Additionally, if this had happened two months later, we would no longer have had a mission doctor available in the Sudan. By then, the new Muslim Sudanese government had issued orders requiring all missionary doctors to leave the country. Large crowds surrounding clinics spoke of the effectiveness of medical work. Fearing that people who came for medical assistance would become Christians, the ruling hierarchy made the decision to expel all medical workers. By doing so, they took the first step toward accomplishing their goal of ridding the country of Christian influence.

Thankful for the guest room that our missionary friends maintained at Logotok, we stayed for five days as Darryl's back began to heal. We returned home with our son on the mend, full of gratitude, after coming so close to losing him. From that point on, we took added precautions with a new appreciation of dangers that surrounded us. Upon arriving home, Harvey immediately bolted down the angle iron to which we tied our mosquito nets.

* * *

The current configuration of our "tin" house required that we all sleep in the living room. Harvey made several little additions to our little "erector set" home. We began using a new bedroom before Harvey found time to pour the concrete floor. Darryl loved that unfinished floor. It gave him a wonderful place to play. He liked to draw pictures in the dirt and then call me to show off his "masterpieces." After viewing one of those drawings in the dirt along with Darryl's explanation of what he had drawn, I told him, "Darryl, you do have an imagination."

I forgot my remark as soon as I made it; Darryl didn't. A year later as Darryl struggled to tell me about something he wanted to accomplish, I asked, "Darryl, where is your imagination?" Without blinking an eye, he ran into our bedroom which now had a concrete floor. He pointed to the place where he had drawn the picture in the dirt a year before and said, "There it is. There's my 'magination."

*   *   *

Darryl often showed surprising determination for his age. He loved to use color books and work dot-to-dot puzzles. These puzzles helped teach him his numbers. One day he asked me a question about a certain dot-to-dot puzzle he tried to complete. I told him, "Darryl, you can't do that one yet because you haven't learned your numbers that far. You need to learn them little by little, and then later you can do the puzzles with larger numbers." With obvious indignation at this demeaning put-down, he replied, "I don't want to learn little by little. I want to learn big by big."

*   *   *

Darryl did some big thinking for a little boy. While still 3 ½, he paged through some photo books. When he saw pictures of his dad as a little boy, Darryl told me that they were pictures of himself. I said, "No, Darryl, those are not pictures of you. They are pictures of Daddy when he was a little boy. You are going to grow up and be a big man someday like Daddy, and then maybe you will have a little boy of your own."

Darryl sat and reflected on what I said for a long time. Then he looked at his legs and responded, "How can these bones get big like Daddy's? I can't get big like Daddy, Mommy, because I just have little bones. I'll get big like Timmy." Tim, at eleven, must have appeared to be a more attainable goal.

*   *   *

Darryl wearing one of his sunsuits

Darryl enjoyed the companionship of our small Alsatian puppy. But he didn't like it when the dog got too friendly and jumped on his back. The more Darryl objected, the more the dog persevered in pestering him with his behavior. Because of Riwoto's constant heat, I dressed Darryl in sunsuits. This left bare areas on his back and the dog's claws scratched him when it jumped on him. We disciplined the dog, but he didn't seem to learn. After one of these episodes, Darryl grabbed the dog by his ears and said, "No, Toots, NO!" But Boots refused to listen.

When Boots jumped on his back again, Darryl decided that he had had enough. Grabbing Boots by the ears, he bit him on his ear so hard that it bled. Although Harvey understood Darryl's frustration, he questioned his response and gave him a spanking. Who ever heard of a boy getting a spanking for biting a dog? However, all of the "discipline" that day seemed to be effective. The dog stopped jumping on Darryl's back; Darryl never bit the dog again.

Darryl with our cat and dog, Boots

*   *   *

One day Harvey wanted Darryl to smile for a picture to send to Grandma. Thinking it might help accomplish his goal, Harvey asked Darryl to say, "Hi Grandma," as he snapped the picture. Stopping a minute to think about this, Darryl questioned, "Is Grandma inside that camera?"

*   *   *

Darryl had a hard time figuring out relationships with his grandparents. He couldn't remember them since he was only fifteen months old when we left America. After we concluded our family time of reading the Bible and praying one day, Darryl asked, "Mommy, does Grandpa hear us when we pray?"

Puzzled, I replied, "No Darryl, we pray to God, and God hears our prayers."

"But when you pray you say, 'Our Father,' and you told me that your father is my grandfather." That took some tall explaining as I attempted to clarify the difference between *our Father in Heaven*, who is God, and *my earthly father*.

25

* * *

Another time we heard that Harvey's grandfather was very sick. We told Darryl that his great-grandfather might die. As happened so often, he thought about that for some time before asking, "What's so great about my grandfather?" This little guy with an analytical mind, had difficulty getting all of these relationships straightened out. We hoped that our upcoming home assignment would enable him to sort things out as he associated faces with the relatives about whom we spoke.

* * *

Darryl loved to pray as we took time for family devotions each day. One day he prayed, "Dear Heavenly Father, help me to sleep this afternoon. And when Daddy comes in to see if I'm sleeping, help me not to blink my eyes like this [blinking a few times so the Lord would know what he meant]. Help me to do all the right things. Do you hear me heavenly Father? Do you hear me Lord? Please help me to be a good boy." Darryl spoke with his Father in heaven when he prayed. Prayer was real to him.

* * *

As Darryl approached his fourth birthday we informed him that we were going to have a new brother or sister in our family. Our other children, along with Darryl, expressed excitement when they heard this news. Without exception, they believed we needed a little sister. Charlotte convinced herself that this baby would be a girl because she had sat on the lawn at her boarding school at night and wished on a star for a sister. And besides that, she had prayed for a sister. Because this would be the sister for whom she had prayed, she insisted that she should also have the privilege of naming her. She wanted to name her Faith, after her good friend at school. We gave Faith the second name of Annette. The day after Faith's birth, the doctor asked Darryl his little sister's name. He replied with great confidence, "It's Face Net."

Dr. Ted teased him about this, saying, "Why don't you just call her Mosquito Net?" Somehow, Darryl missed the humor, rejecting that name as a bad idea.

* * *

Some friends expressed surprise at Darryl's rapid adjustment to the change in our family. He didn't act jealous of the attention diverted to his new sister; he even seemed quite happy to give up his place on my lap when we traveled. Darryl enjoyed the role of big brother and moved out of his screen crib with great enthusiasm. Now, grown up enough to sleep in his big brothers' bed on the screen porch delighted him. Except, with his older brothers away at school, he seemed untroubled that he had to sleep on that porch all alone.

He drew the line in one area. Darryl loved to be called *Punkie* by his dad. When Darryl heard Dad call baby Faith, *Punkie*, he reacted with vigor. With great emphasis he stated, "Faith isn't big enough to be a Punkie!"

* * *

Perhaps because of decreased attention, Darryl exhibited another side of his character during these transitional days. While home from school on vacation, his older sister and brothers watched dumfounded as he banged his head on the cement floor because he didn't get his way in something. A huge, blue bump rose on his forehead. His older siblings looked on this as very unintelligent behavior. It left a lasting memory of a young life that needed to be shaped and molded by the discipline of his parents and God's gracious ongoing work in his life.

* * *

At five years of age, Darryl loved to write and draw so Harvey made him a chalkboard. When he realized that the chalkboard belonged to him, he grabbed a piece of chalk and printed his name. He also loved to have someone read to him and took every opportunity to look at books on his own. He revealed an affinity for books and learning early in life. Harvey took a telling photo of him at age three sitting on a potty as he looked with great intensity at a book entitled, *Childhood Behavior.* The book did not contain a single picture. We never did understand his serious contemplation of that enlightening tome.

Darryl with his chalkboard on his 5ᵗʰ birthday

*   *   *

After completing our normal four-year term of service, we returned to America for home assignment. We received reentry visas from the Sudan government, however, the tense atmosphere made us question if we would be allowed to return. This made planning difficult. We packed some things to take on the plane with us. Other things we packed to be sent to us in America if the Sudanese government prohibited our return. Certain items were designated for friends to sell or give away if the door to reentry closed. Indeed, we were expelled from the country while we were on home assignment. We never saw most of those things again.

Chapter 4

TRANSITION TO AMERICA

Darryl anxiously awaited the beginning of school. Harvey took him to enroll him in kindergarten. As they left the school yard that day, Darryl looked up at his dad with a troubled look on his face and asked, "Daddy, what were all those toys in that school room for?"

"Those are for you to play with in kindergarten, Darryl."

Aghast, Darryl replied, "I'm not going to go to school to play. I'm going to school to learn to read!"

During the school year, someone set up a play telephone system in Darryl's kindergarten classroom. It connected a "store" in one corner to another area of the room. One day the telephone system wouldn't work. Darryl liked to stick close to his brother Ray and often observed him repairing some electrical or other gadget. This gave Darryl the belief that anything that didn't work could be made to work with a little tinkering. He dismantled that play phone system, put it back together, and made it work! He told us about his repair job when he got home from school, but then added, "When it was time to go home I unfixed it though, because I wanted to see if the afternoon kindergarten kids were smart enough to fix it up again." I never did hear the outcome of that one.

In November, we received word of our expulsion from the Sudan. This didn't surprise us; we saw clear indications before we left the Sudan that we might not be allowed to return.

During our early days of home assignment we had been wrestling with another question—the responsibility of meeting the needs of the maturing children God had entrusted to us as they approached high school age concerned us. We spent much time in prayer about this and about the simmering situation in the Sudan. We asked God for wisdom and found peace in remembering that God had called us to work in the Sudan. Since no new missionaries could gain access to the southern Sudan, Harvey and I agreed that we should continue our work there as long as God kept the door open for us. If He allowed us to return, we could trust Him to enable us to meet the needs of our children. If, on the other hand, the government denied us permission to return to the Sudan, we further agreed that we should step aside from overseas missionary service until our older children completed these critical years of their lives. When word of our expulsion came from the Sudan our decision had been made, and we recognized that God had set a new course for our family.

In a unique way, God had already begun to make provision for this new phase in our lives. As we settled into life in America, we needed to prepare for the chilling effects of a Turlock winter. After living in the hot climate of the Sudan for four years, we didn't have clothing for our growing family for these cooler temperatures. Harvey decided to find work to enable us to buy the necessary warm clothing. My brother, Wilbur, one of our most committed supporters as we served on the field, broke ground on an expansion project of his feed mill on what had been our old family farm. As Harvey shared his desire to find work, Wilbur offered him a job.

Promoted to manager after a year on the job at Merrill Milling, Harvey oversaw the installation of a new automated feed mixing system. He also participated in many evening meetings at our church. This meant that I occupied the driver's seat at home a lot more than I desired. The mix of three high schoolers, a six-year old, and a two-year old created the need for a good disciplinarian. After losing little Donny at birth in Africa, I found it difficult to carry through with needed discipline. Harvey had taken responsibility for most of this, but his new commitments often kept him away from home when disciplinary needs arose. I struggled with the fact that I *must* discipline our children. They needed consistent discipline to become the men and women that God wanted them to be.

Then, in my daily Bible reading I came to the book of 1 Samuel. I spent much time reading and meditating on those opening chapters. God reproved the priest, Eli, for neglecting to restrain his sons when they did things that displeased God. Conviction gripped me as I read the question God asked Eli, "Why do you honor your sons more than me [by allowing them to disobey me]?" (1 Samuel 2:29b NIV) Reading on, the dire warning of verse 33 stirred my heart to the depths, "Every one of you that I do not cut off from my altar will be spared only to blind your eyes with tears and to grieve your heart, and all your descendants will die in the prime of life."

God reconfirmed this warning given to Eli. In the middle of the night, He spoke to the young boy Samuel who served in the temple, saying, "I told him that I would judge his family forever because of the sin he knew about; his sons made themselves contemptible, and he failed to restrain them" (1 Samuel 3:13 NIV). Tears streamed down my cheeks as I read these passages. I recognized that God entrusted me with the responsibility of teaching each of our children to obey, not only us, but of even greater importance, God. I knew that God was speaking to me. If I didn't instruct these precious children, disciplining when necessary, they would suffer loss in their lives; beyond that, Harvey and I would share in that suffering and loss.

Around this time, Darryl again demonstrated that strong will evident in his early life. Harvey's absence from home many evenings seemed to encourage Darryl to test my reaction to increased disobedience. He had grown into a strong, muscular kid. I recognized and accepted my God-given responsibility, but I sometimes found it hard to handle him. On several occasions I asked one of his older siblings to hold him down so I could give him the spanking that he needed for his defiance.

An incident brought to my attention by one of our neighbors spurred me on to do what I needed to. Congenial, even in first grade, Darryl liked to visit with people on his way home from school. True to form, he stopped one afternoon to talk to our next-door neighbor. After talking to Darryl for a while she said, "Well Darryl, maybe you had better hurry home, because your mother might wonder where you are and scold you for being late."

Darryl replied, "Oh, my mom's not that way."

She passed the incident on to me and her words jolted me into thinking, "Oh, oh! Maybe I should be more 'that way.'" That drove me back to those same early chapters of 1 Samuel. I spent more hours thinking about and meditating on those passages. As I read futher, dawning realization rumbled through my consciousness. God not only warned Eli, He did what He said He would do. Eli and his sons all died on the same day. If I wanted God's best for us and for our children, I had to trust God and discipline as the Lord expected me to do. God blessed that resolve, and we saw a difference. An added confirmation that God had spoken to me during those days came to light years later as Faith told me the other side of an incident I had known only from my perspective.

Darryl (7 years old) and Faith (3) played in the backyard. The previous week Harvey saw them hanging on the clothesline and told them not to do that anymore. He recognized the potential danger to them and the possibility that they might ruin the clothesline. He let them know that they would get a spanking if they chose to do it again. Aware of his warning, I looked out and saw them having a great time hanging on the clothesline. I called out, "Darryl and Faith, come in the house. Didn't Daddy tell you that you would get a spanking if you played on the clothesline like that?"

"Yes," they responded in chorus.

"I'm sorry, but Daddy warned you, and I'm going to have to give you a spanking." After they each received a spanking, they returned to the backyard to play. I was amazed when I checked on them a few minutes later and again found them both hanging on the clothesline as if I had said or done nothing to correct them.

"OK, kids, come in the house. I'm going to have to give you another spanking. Why didn't you obey me?" They took their punishment and returned to the backyard.

I really couldn't believe my eyes when I looked out a short time later and found those two little rascals doing the same thing for the third time. "Well, kids, I guess you still haven't learned your lesson, so I'll have to give you another spanking,"

Years later Faith told me that as they went out the door that third time, Darryl said, "You know, Faith, I don't think we'd better do that again." Although it took three spankings, they remembered the lesson learned. I thanked God for prompting me to show my love for our children by obeying Him in providing needed, consistent discipline. "No discipline seems pleasant at the time, but painful. Later on, however, it produces a harvest of righteousness and peace for those who have been trained by it" (Hebrews 12:11 NIV).

God was teaching me in other ways too. I have always had an interest in medical things and I started listening to the soap opera, *General Hospital.* Our older children usually arrived home after the program ended but school let out an hour early once a month. On those days, Charlotte liked to join me in front of the TV. One day as she sat with me, they showed three different situations portraying illicit sexual relationships within a short time span. As I watched my daughter sitting beside me and lapping this stuff up, I thought, "What in the world am I doing?"

Conviction gripped me; God prompted my action. I reached over and turned the TV off, saying, "Charlotte, this is no kind of a program for you to be watching. It isn't good for you to see this kind of trash, and it isn't good for me either."

Charlotte objected. She wanted to see the outcome of the story. Convinced that I had made the right decision, I told her, "I'm sorry, but it has to be that way."

I felt convicted and regretted my earlier blindness. My careless choice led my teenaged daughter in a wrong direction because "I had an interest in medical things." I never listened to that program again. That experience made me more selective about what I looked at on TV. As a mother, I realized that I also needed to learn discipline.

Although our family hadn't spent a lot of time watching TV, now we took a new approach. We made it a practice to watch a few carefully chosen programs together. At the conclusion of a program, we took time to discuss what we saw. We asked the children to note anything that conflicted with our Christian values. We discussed their responses and added our observations. This not only helped our children learn Christian values, but also provided tools for them to differentiate between Godly values and values of the world.

Soon after Darryl turned eight and Faith neared four, another precious daughter, Susan Irene, joined our family. This addition to our family meant that we needed another vehicle. We could not fit our tribe into the one we owned. After we brought our *new* used car home, Ray and Tim checked it out with their dad. With the hood up, they looked at the engine. Climbing up beside them, Darryl cast a practiced eye over this new wonder. Gazing in, he asked, "Where's the baby food can?"

Someone asked, "What in the world are you talking about, Darryl?"

Then they remembered. Our truck in Africa had a baby food can that covered the oil filler tube. We had lost our oil cap somewhere along an African dirt road. Harvey, or perhaps Ray, discovered that a baby food can made a good and tight-fitting cover. Darryl still remembered how a "real" engine looked even though we had left the Sudan three years before. We often marveled at the sharp mind God gave this little fellow.

Darryl loved to go to church and wrote the following assessment of primary church:

> I would like to tell you how much I like Primary Church. This is what we do in Primary Church. First we read someone's Christian story. Then we sing this song:
>
> > This is God's house, and He is here today.
> > He hears us when we sing and listens when we pray.
>
> Then we pray. Then we bring the offering. Then we have a story that Mrs. Lindquist brings. Then we pray again. I really like Primary Church.

Darryl learned to read early and enjoyed reading his Bible. He not only read but spent time in deep thought about what he read. I went into his room one day to talk to him. Even though he was only seven at the time, he looked at me and asked, "Mother, can I just be alone? I want to think." I complied with his request and left him to himself. I wondered many times, "What was he thinking about so deeply?"

As Darryl continued to grow, his older siblings deemed him old enough to help them with the dishes at night. He willingly joined in drying the dishes, but now one of his "mentors" couldn't resist teasing him, "Darryl, don't overwork yourself." Darryl smiled and replied, "Oh, I'm used to overwork." I'm not sure if he understood their comment or why they laughed at his response, but by cheerfully helping with the dishes he silenced his critics—up to a point. They didn't forget his remark and in coming months continued to parrot back to him, "Oh, I'm used to overwork"—at appropriate and, sometimes, inappropriate times.

As time wore on, Harvey felt drawn to return to full-time Christian service. He shared these feelings with my brother. Wilbur hated to think of him leaving but did not want to do anything to keep Harvey from doing what the Lord wanted him to do. Soon after Harvey shared his desire with

Wilbur, a teaching position opened at Western Bible Institute in Morrison, Colorado. Harvey flew to Colorado to learn about the school and to meet with the president, the faculty, and the official board of the school. Darryl had a hard time waiting for Dad to return home. When we met the plane at our small, nearby airport in Modesto, Darryl called out as Harvey walked into the baggage area, "Dad, are we going?"

"Yes, we're going."

So Harvey left his job as manager of Merrill Milling and started a new career as professor, near Denver, Colorado. Since Western Bible Institute was a small school, Harvey agreed to become head of the Missions Department, teach missions and Bible, and to serve as Dean of Students. He took on a very full plate.

Charlotte and Ray remained in California to return to Biola College, but Tim experienced a painful transition. He had to change schools for his senior year in high school severing relationships with many friends. He also lost the companionship of his older brother. Tim did receive a consolation prize; he got to drive our car most of the way to Denver, a responsibility he carried out with excellence. Harvey drove a U-Haul truck, and I had my hands full trying to meet the needs of our little sixteen-month old Susan. Consequently, Tim's source of enjoyment fulfilled a tremendous need.

Darryl left behind a special friend his age in Turlock too. Billy Barnett lived a few houses down the street. Darryl voiced concern about Billy because he didn't go to church. He invited Billy to go with us to Sunday School and church, and we often heard him talking with Billy about Jesus. Before we left California, Darryl gave his nice, big Bible story book to Billy. Many years later, we found out that Billy had become a Christian because Darryl had introduced him to Christ.

Chapter 5

CAMPUS LIFE IN COLORADO

*M*oving to Colorado proved to be a challenging experience. We gave up our beautiful California home and moved into a restructured World War II barracks. It retained the stark look and feel of an army barracks in spite of remodeling. Although previously converted into a house, now we worked hard to make it a home. Providing solace in this adjustment, we enjoyed an incredible view as we looked out in any direction from our home. Positioned in the foothills of the majestic Rocky Mountains, beauty surrounded the campus of Western Bible Institute.

Our family at Western Bible Institute

Superb weather welcomed us at the end of July, but it didn't last long. Soon after the children started school in September a huge, early snowstorm engulfed us. The bus provided by Jefferson County Schools never arrived. Deep snow prohibited safe travel. Wet snow had broken down power lines and cut off electricity. We ate a cold breakfast in a frigid house. We had heard about Colorado's unpredictable weather; now we felt it. The afternoon before the storm, I worked vigorously in 85 degree weather, washing and shining my windows. As I worked, threatening clouds moved in and covered the sky; the wind began to howl and the temperature rapidly plummeted. Unbearable cold enveloped me as snow began to fall. Even then, I never dreamed that we would awaken to find ourselves immobilized by a deep blanket of snow. But, after we cleared our doors to enable us to exit, the kids had a great day playing in the snow.

The bright side of a snowy day!

* * *

In spite of careful planning, Western retained a Spartan look. A huge barren field abutting a road separated us from the exclusive subdivision called Willowbrook. Darryl enjoyed playing there after we settled into our new home. One day after spending an afternoon with a friend, he remarked in a matter-of-fact manner, "I feel so sorry for those kids living in Willowbrook."

Shocked by his statement, I replied, "You feel sorry for those Willowbrook kids? What in the world for? They have everything they could ever want."

Darryl, showing wisdom beyond that of his mother, said, "Yes, Mother, they have everything, but because they have so much they can't enjoy any of it. They don't think anything is special. When you and Dad get us any little thing we can really enjoy it, because we don't have a lot." I could not help but be in awe at the depth of insight God had built into this ten-year-old boy.

We saw that spiritual perception in other areas of Darryl's life too. Married students lived in remodeled barracks comparable to ours. Several of those families had children near Darryl's age, and he often played with them. One family had two boys. Before coming to Western, those boys had developed considerable skill in fighting and loved to show off their expertise. One day, one of them poked Darryl hoping to provoke a fight. The boys asked him why he refused to hit back. Darryl responded that he did not fight back because the Bible says that if someone hits you, you should turn the other cheek and let them hit that one too.

They retorted, "What would you do if they did hit the other cheek?"

Darryl's quiet answer seemed to catch them off guard and stopped the attack. "Then maybe I would get a chance to tell them about Jesus."

* * *

In Darryl's fourth grade class at Bear Creek Elementary School, one of his teachers introduced evolution. In a careful but intentional manner Darryl raised his hand. "What do you want Darryl?" his teacher asked.

Darryl responded, "I'm sorry, but I can't agree with what you're saying."

"Why is that, Darryl?"

"Because I believe the Bible."

Feeling certain that she had an adequate answer, his teacher responded, "That's all right, Darryl, you can believe the Bible and evolution too."

Without a moment's hesitation, Darryl whipped out a New Testament from his shirt pocket and replied, "I can't accept evolution because of what it says in Hebrews 11:3." He began to read in a slow and deliberate voice, "Through faith we understand that the worlds were framed by the word of God, so that things which are seen were not made of things which do appear." He added, "Evolution contradicts this."

I don't know if Darryl won his argument but that teacher did not bring up the subject of evolution again throughout the remainder of the year.

* * *

Darryl and one of his friends enjoyed hiking. One day they hiked up into the foothills adjacent to Western. From their vantage point they could see the school campus and Willowbrook as well as a wide area beyond the campus. As they enjoyed this beautiful and awe-inspiring sight, they discovered company—unexpected and unwanted company. First they heard, then they saw, a huge rattlesnake showing resentment that someone had invaded his territory. They ran off, thankful that the poisonous rattler chose not to follow them. In fact, they didn't slow down until they got back to the campus. When I heard their story, I breathed a prayer of thanks for God's protection of my son in a situation out of my control.

* * *

After living at Western for a year, we moved to another house across the campus adjacent to Western's radio station. We believed the floor plan of this house better suited our family's needs. Western owned generous acreage for its campus, and the campus property line ran close to our new home. Soon after we moved, the man who owned the vacant, barren property adjacent to the campus expressed outrage that some children living at Western climbed over the barbed wire fence and played in his vacant field. Infuriated, he delivered an ultimatum. If he found anyone from Western on his property he would shoot him.

This irrational but serious threat prompted us to warn Darryl not to set foot on the grounds of this intimidating neighbor. I further told Darryl that if he didn't obey he would be confined to the yard around our house for a whole weekend. Engrossed in play with some of his friends a few days later, Darryl forgot my warning. I think the boys saw some wild flowers and climbed over the fence to pick some extra pretty ones for their mothers. When I saw him in that forbidden territory, I called him home and stated, "Darryl, you know we told you not to go onto that neighbor's land. Why did you go?"

"I'm sorry, Mom. I guess I just forgot."

"I'm sorry too, Darryl," I answered, "but we told you not to cross over into that field; we also told you not to go anywhere near that fence. You know, we don't want to give our neighbor an excuse to do a dumb thing like shoot someone. Now, as I warned you, you'll have to stay in our yard for the rest of the weekend."

Dreading such a bleak weekend, Darryl countered with a suggestion of his own, "Mom, can't you please give me a spanking instead so I can go play with the boys?"

I held firm, "No, Darryl, I said that you would have to stay in the yard." In spite of his continued begging, I refused to budge. That alternative punishment hurt him far more than any spanking.

*   *   *

Darryl worked hard in school and out of school. He played the violin and participated in the school orchestra. He also took piano lessons, demonstrating extraordinary musical ability.

His school offered an outdoor lab for sixth graders. We couldn't afford to send him, but someone found a scholarship for him. Despite the cold weather, the children took pleasure in this outdoor camping experience in the mountains. Children attending the lab learned about different trees, insects, and conservation techniques. Darryl loved it. Soon after he returned from outdoor lab, however, he developed a swollen gland on the left side of his jaw. We knew that it couldn't be mumps because he had had them on both sides of his face a few months earlier. The problem persisted so we took him to see our family doctor. Dr. Kurtz first tested him for mononucleosis, then for lymphoma. Both tests came back negative. Darryl continued to have problems and I felt very uneasy.

Chapter 6

A PAPER BOY IN LAKEWOOD

*A*t this time, God blessed us again with a house of our own in nearby Lakewood, Colorado. Moving to Lakewood changed our lifestyle. Now Harvey had to travel ten miles to work each day instead of walking across the campus. I had to take Harvey to work whenever I needed the car—we only had one.

Darryl saw our change in location as an opportunity and lost no time in taking advantage of it. He called Denver newspapers in search of an open route and got a job with the Rocky Mountain News. As soon as he knew that he had the job, this twelve-year old came to me and said, "Mom, you don't need to buy me any more clothes. Since I'll be making my own money I'll buy my own clothes now." He did—except when he received gifts of clothing for Christmas or his birthday.

He enunciated that independent spirit and commitment to take responsibility in the way he carried out his new job. Darryl set his own alarm for 4:30 AM. Jumping out of bed, he threw on his clothes and went into the cold garage to roll his papers. Packing them in his big canvas news bag slung across his bike handlebars, he cycled over a mile up and down hills to where his route began. This worked out fine in pleasant weather but rain and snow sometimes changed the picture. On several occasions, icy snow accumulated on his bike tires and wedged against the bike frame until his wheels no longer turned. With wheels frozen in place, Darryl had no alternative but to walk home and ask for help from Dad. After they retrieved his bike and papers from their snowy prison, they completed his route for the day by car. Such setbacks never deterred Darryl from trying to do it on his own the following day.

Darryl worked hard to please his customers. It encouraged him when he succeeded and was rewarded with tips at the end of the month. That, in turn, motivated him to try even harder. Concerned about papers getting water-soaked, he came up with the idea of wrapping his papers in plastic. Although commonly done today, he pioneered the concept for his customers. Putting feet to his idea, he went to our nearby grocery store and asked to buy a roll of imprinted plastic bags used for vegetables. The store sold him the bags at a bargain price—glad to get free advertising. Wrapping papers in plastic not only protected them from rain, it also kept them together in the fierce winds of the area. Papers inserted in plastic bags and closed with a rubber bands rarely moved from where he placed them.

When one of Darryl's more difficult customers moved away, he gave Darryl his poodle named Snowball. Since Snowball had a weird personality, we wondered if this customer had an ulterior motive in giving Darryl the dog. Did he do it to show appreciation or disdain? Had Darryl's service somehow failed to meet his expectations? In spite of Snowball's strange behavior, Darryl enjoyed him. The dog liked to get under an upholstered chair where he snarled and tried to attack anyone walking by. We used a yardstick to push him out from under the chair. Once away from the chair, his aggressive attitude melted away. Snowball packed quite a punch for such a little ball of fur.

* * *

Darryl excelled as a student at Dunstan Junior High School and enjoyed playing his violin in the school orchestra. His outgoing personality enabled him to make many friends. He enjoyed school—both the opportunity to learn and the interaction with friends. Jefferson County Schools touted their position as the most progressive school district in the United States. From our standpoint, their "progressive education" placed constant pressure on our personal and Christian value system.

In seeking to address one area that concerned us, we had Darryl excused from the sex education class. We preferred to teach these values in our own home. A few days later, Darryl shared an experience that reinforced the wisdom of our decision. During lunch hour, he saw a bunch of boys absorbed in a book and displaying raucous laughter. He assumed they had a Playboy magazine but, instead, discovered their laughter emanated from pictures and text in their sex education class textbook.

*　　*　　*

We attended Judson Baptist Church in Denver. During their annual Missionary Conference they challenged members to make a faith promise for missions. Darryl decided to participate. After thinking and praying about this, he made a large commitment for the year, an amount greater than his potential earnings enabled him to pay. When we questioned him concerning the wisdom of making such a large commitment, he responded, "This is the only way my giving will really be faith. If I only commit to give what I know I can earn, that wouldn't really be faith." He wanted to allow God to do something for him that he couldn't do for himself. As parents, we wondered how this would work out. Nevertheless, we didn't think we should interfere in a decision Darryl had made after serious thought and prayer.

*　　*　　*

Darryl's jaw continued to swell up periodically after the original episode when he returned from outdoor lab. This often occurred either when he had a cold or when the weather turned very cold. The doctor told us that very small ducts in that gland sometimes cause trouble if they get blocked. He further suggested that Darryl would have to learn to live with this. Darryl seldom complained about the pain, but occasionally made me aware of it by remarks such as, "Mom, my ears (or some other facial feature) are hurting." These incidents continued to trouble me and I wondered if the doctor really understood the cause.

*   *   *

Darryl had a good friend at school named Peter Fowler. Peter didn't come from a Christian home and had never gone to church. Darryl often talked to him about Jesus and urged him to believe that when Christ died on the cross He paid the penalty for Peter's sin. He explained that trusting Christ for salvation would free Peter from eternal punishment. Peter contemplated this, but did not make a decision to follow Christ. This concerned Darryl and he often prayed for his friend. One day Peter asked Darryl, "Why have you been trying so hard to convert me? I'm just too materialistic to believe."

"You're my friend, Peter, and I don't want you to go to hell."

Somewhat subdued, Peter answered, "Darryl, I really do appreciate your concern." In spite of being bothered by his directness, Peter continued to value Darryl's friendship and expressed in a note to Darryl:

> To Darryl Stranske who is trustworthy, loyal, helpful, courteous, kind, obedient, friendly, cheerful, brave, clean, thrifty, brave again, and reverent. He is a good friend who has shown me a lot of what is wrong and right in this world and I thank you Darryl.
>
> Peter Fowler

*   *   *

Darryl always carried his New Testament in his pocket. Never afraid to tell people about Jesus, he would take it out at any time to show a friend what God's Word said. This enticed some of his schoolmates to make fun of him and attempt to make him angry. One time a boy grabbed Darryl's New Testament out of his pocket and slung it down the school hallway as far as it would go. A student who saw this happen told us later that Darryl just turned to his tormentor, smiled, and said, "Thank you." Then he walked down the hall to retrieve his property. Darryl's refusal to get angry often took the fun out of teasing him.

* * *

Harvey's graduation from University of Colorado

For two years, Harvey had worked toward a master's degree in linguistics at the University of Colorado in Boulder along with carrying a full teaching load at Western Bible Institute. As school closed for both Harvey and the children, we decided we all needed a break. We packed our tent and spent two refreshing weeks at Mesa Verde in Colorado and Carlsbad Caverns in New Mexico.

Setting up the tent on our vacation

When we returned, the Rocky Mountain News offered Darryl the route in proximity to our home. He no longer had to carry his heavy load of papers that long distance to the beginning of his route. Darryl had ninety-seven customers on his new route, and he determined to build it up to at least one hundred. A contest sponsored by the paper to get new customers helped him exceed his goal. He signed up more than six new customers and, as a reward, received a day at Elitch's Amusement Park in Denver. Several of Darryl's friends achieved the same reward so they spent a day together at the amusement park.

Darryl loved the roller coaster and kept going on it over and over. While waiting for one ride to start, his friend in the seat next to him anxiously pulled on the bar that would soon lower across their laps. Darryl had leaned forward to look at something. The operator hit the release and the bar struck Darryl across the left side of his face—the same side of his face where his gland had given him problems. When he returned home, he told us about the incident and said it still hurt a lot. Since I couldn't see a bruise on his face nor any other evidence of an injury, I suggested, "Maybe it will feel better after a good night's sleep."

The following day we decided to explore a part of Colorado that we had not seen—Canyon City and the grandeur of Royal Gorge. Darryl usually relished such a trip, but he did not enjoy this one. He became nauseated and vomited. It was impossible for him to enjoy anything. Of course, this put a damper on our outing. He began to feel a little better when we returned home that evening. At the time, we didn't associate his accident on the roller coaster with his illness, but later the relationship seemed apparent.

Darryl started having frequent attacks of pain in his gland, often brought on by excitement of any kind. Our family enjoyed playing table games on Friday evenings, but this often resulted in pain for him. His gland enlarged, pressed on his ear, and caused severe earaches. His gums on that side of his mouth swelled and made his teeth ache. Sometimes his gums became numb. Our family physician opted for a second opinion and sent Darryl to see Dr. Dragel, an Ear, Nose, and Throat Specialist.

Darryl's attacks continued to get worse, but always occurred either on weekends or concurrent with the doctor's closed office. The swelling always decreased by the time we could get an appointment, so Dr. Dragel never observed the symptoms about which we spoke. Later, we learned from a worker in his office that Dr. Dragel concluded Darryl had a psychological problem. Suggesting that Darryl's problem may stem from a nerve, Dr. Dragel referred him to a neurologist, Dr. Miller. On our second appointment, the neurologist asked me in private, "What is Darryl really like? At home, I mean?"

I answered, "Doctor Miller, if you're asking me if he is making this up in his mind, let me tell you about him. This boy gets up at 4:30 AM by using his own alarm clock. He rolls newspapers and goes out on his bike, even in freezing weather, to deliver the papers. He works hard and doesn't complain. If he ever says something hurts, I am sure, IT HURTS!" I wanted to make it clear that Darryl didn't have psychological problems.

Dr. Miller decided that the pain centered in the mandibular area and gave Darryl some medicine to calm those nerves. That didn't help. He next recommended taking Darryl to a dentist to check his teeth and gums. But Darryl inherited the teeth of his father and had excellent teeth. He never had even one filling. The dentist found nothing wrong with his teeth, but he felt his gums did look abnormal. He suggested that, perhaps, Darryl didn't brush his teeth well. Knowing Darryl, we did not consider this a possibility. Increasingly, we believed that the real problem eluded all of our doctors.

The next time we returned to Dr. Miller, he had conferred with Dr. Dragel and decided to send Darryl to Swedish Hospital for tests. Darryl entered the hospital on December 2. They took chest x-rays and gave him an arteriogram, a procedure in which technicians inject dye into an area of the body to enhance x-rays. They took a spinal tap to check for the possibility of leukemia or other diseases. They did a pneumoencephalogram, a procedure that involved injecting air into his spine. Following this, they instructed him to lie flat on his back for many hours to avoid getting a severe headache; still he got a very bad headache. He returned home on December 6. All of the test results came back negative. The doctor concluded that when he suffered the blow across his face at the amusement park it damaged a nerve. He gave him medication that, he hoped, would relax this nerve.

A week later, Darryl experienced another severe attack during the night. His lip turned numb on the left side. Yet another time, I gave him medicine when an attack appeared imminent. This enabled him to relax so that he did not have a full-blown attack. The following day the doctor told us to send him back to school. We did, but after spending only a few hours there, Darryl phoned home to tell us he had a terrible headache. We brought him home and called his doctor to explain what happened. The doctor recommended that someone take Darryl out for a good hike. So Harvey and Darryl enjoyed a long but easy hike. No sooner had they returned home than Darryl's gland began to swell again. This time it remained enlarged.

Again, the attack occurred on a Friday causing us frustration once more. We tried to see the doctor but had to wait until Monday during office hours. Then, for the first time, Dr. Dragel saw what we had talked about for many months. He exclaimed, "The sub maxillary gland is the problem! It must be removed."

The doctor scheduled surgery for Darryl at Porter Hospital for December 20. The gland proved to be very large, spongy and full of scars, but the pathology report again came back negative for cancer or anything else.

Darryl shared a hospital room with a very frightened young boy scheduled for a tonsillectomy the next day. Even after all of those weeks of struggle, Darryl continued to live out what he believed so deeply and talked to this boy about God and how God helped him. He shared that God could also give him peace as he faced his operation. The boy later told his mother that he wished he knew about the Bible the way Darryl did.

Since Darryl had a sweet and uncomplaining attitude, hospital workers liked him and often congregated in his room. We thanked God for Darryl's pleasant disposition in the face of many uncomfortable tests and an undefined illness that continued for such a long time.

Chapter 7

THE NEW YEAR BEGINS WITH ENVELOPING GLOOM

Darryl returned home from the hospital the morning of Christmas Eve. On that day, I made the decision to burn our well-preserved Christmas tree candle and we began our festive, family Christmas weekend. But at the end of that wonderful Christmas week I took Darryl to see Dr. Kurtz again and received the disquieting report that he appeared to have some kind of lymphoma. Then Charlotte, Ray and Tim returned to college which added to the somber quietness of our home. The old year faded into history; the new year began, filled with disturbing questions.

Sitting alone on our living room couch, I gazed out through the picture window. The young maple tree in our front yard stood in the cold snow-covered ground, stripped of its leaves and quivering in the wind. My eyes filled with tears. As I focused on that shivering tree, I too trembled; a myriad of mind-boggling eventualities caused my heart to race. In tune with the weather, I felt a chill as I thought of what this new year might bring into our lives.

Darryl, Faith, Susan, and I in front of our Lakewood house
after a snowstorm. Behind us stands the young maple tree.

Harvey walked into the room with his Bible in hand. We had finished
breakfast and prepared for our daily family Bible reading and prayer. "OK,"
he said, calling our children, "let's all sit together on the couch this morning."
On this first day of a new year, Harvey asked each one to share what he or
she wanted God to do in our lives during the coming year. I sat there, totally
dumbstruck, my whole being crying out in chaotic turmoil. Thinking anew
about our lives so up in the air and distraught with concern about Darryl's
health, Harvey's question only served to flood my eyes with tears. Then
I remembered our children sitting with us and wondered what they were
thinking as they saw me break out in tears this way. None of them knew the
ominous news that Dr. Kurtz had shared with me and had little inkling of
the impending storm looming on the horizon. As my thoughts raged out of
control, Harvey began to read I Thessalonians 4:13-18:

> But I would not have you to be ignorant, brethren, concerning
> them which are asleep, that ye sorrow not, even as others which
> have no hope. For if we believe that Jesus died and rose again, even

so them also which sleep in Jesus will God bring with him. For this we say unto you by the word of the Lord, that we which are alive and remain unto the coming of the Lord shall not prevent them which are asleep. For the Lord himself shall descend from heaven with a shout, with the voice of the archangel, and with the trump of God: and the dead in Christ shall rise first: Then we which are alive and remain shall be caught up together with them in the clouds, to meet the Lord in the air: and so shall we ever be with the Lord. Wherefore comfort one another with these words.

After he read those concluding words, "Wherefore comfort [encourage] one another with these words," Harvey suggested that we memorize this hope-filled portion of scripture. So we sat repeating phrases to help us learn the passage. I dutifully restated those words. While my ears heard the wonderful promises, my brain refused to appropriate the message. Instead of the words encouraging me, they seemed to tantalize me and I felt like I couldn't hold back the tears. My mind asserted that to arise with Christ when He comes, a person has to die and not continue to be a part of our lives. How could I accept the thought of that separation?

Question after question flooded my thoughts. Would this son whom I loved so deeply be taken from us during this year? With incredible effort I pulled myself together for the sake of those three precious children observing me on our living room couch that frigid New Year's morning.

With the New Year's weekend behind, Darryl entered Porter Hospital for scheduled tests. The girls returned to school and Harvey left for work. The following morning the ringing phone interrupted my wandering thoughts. What were they doing with Darryl now? Had any of the tests revealed his problem? I answered the phone and heard the voice of Dr. Kurtz. Numbness enveloped me. I slipped into a chair as the meaning of his message gripped the deepest recesses of my being. No! This couldn't be. These kinds of things just happen to other people.

"We have looked at Darryl's x-rays taken this morning," Dr. Kurtz began. "We found his left lung filled with fluid except for a small circle about the size of a dollar. A month ago his x-rays revealed no fluid, so this has happened very quickly. We expect fluid to invade the other lung also, and of course, that is all he has with which to breathe."

"Isn't there anything you can do?" I pled desparately.

Dr. Kurtz paused for a moment and then replied, "We can and will drain the fluid, but it will come back again. Mrs. Stranske, Darryl probably only has a month or two to live at best. If you have wanted to do something special or know of a place that Darryl would enjoy, I advise you to go now. I am so sorry to have to give you this message, but that is the way it is."

Almost out of context, I asked, "Will Darryl be going back to school?"

Hesitating, Dr. Kurtz responded, "There really wouldn't be much use for him to go back."

"Should we tell him what you have said?" I queried.

I noticed a long pause before our caring doctor answered, "No, don't tell him anything until we have a definitive diagnosis. We hope to have that by the end of the week."

Overwhelmed, I stated the only words I could muster, "Thank you, Dr. Kurtz."

Grief consumed me. With tears flowing, I looked at the calendar hanging over our desk. January 5, Darryl's fourteenth birthday. Harvey, Faith, Susan and I had planned to go to the hospital in the evening with a birthday cake and gifts to help Darryl celebrate another year of life. As a new year began for any of our children I often reminisced about the year that had passed, but to a greater extent, I focused on the year ahead. I had dreamed of the joy of seeing this son grow to maturity. He was so gifted scholastically and musically. God had blessed him with a special and pleasing personality. Now, with the doctor's message sinking in, I had little reason for dreaming of a future for Darryl.

My body trembled as I dialed the number of my husband's office. When he answered, I passed on the devastating news I had received. We agonized together recognizing that our lives would never be the same. Thoughtfully, Harvey responded, "Honey, I'm coming home."

As Harvey arrived home we continued to grieve together as we faced the prospect of coming days. A ringing doorbell broke into our sorrowful discussion. Marie, our next-door neighbor, had seen Harvey come home at an unusual hour. She knew that we expected results of Darryl's tests so she rushed over. Seeing our subdued manner, she could hardly catch her breath before inquiring, "Did you get word about Darryl?"

"Well Marie," I responded, "this is Darryl's fourteenth birthday and according to the doctor's report it will probably be his last. He says that Darryl has only a month or two to live." Shaken, Marie groaned, "Oh, Evadene and Harvey, I'm so sorry to hear that. He is just one of the nicest kids around." Marie mourned with us as she returned home.

We felt confused and disoriented as we tried to decide what we should do next. When our daughters got home from school, we all went shopping to try to find a suitable birthday gift for Darryl. What a dilemma. How could we choose a worthwhile gift for someone who had so little time to live? We searched without results for something—not knowing what to get. Finally, we spotted a craft store. "Oh look," I said, as I spied a string art kit with a large roadrunner bird begging to be assembled. We settled on the purchase. Darryl loved to create things with his hands, and we agreed that he would enjoy this while he had to remain quiet when he returned home.

Since he had to spend his birthday in such a dismal environment, we stopped at the hospital for a while in the late afternoon to cheer him up. As often happened, Darryl displayed his usual happy face and cheered us up instead. His circumstances didn't dampen his spirits at all. We told him that we would return right after supper. I didn't feel like cooking nor did we want to waste time that we could spend with Darryl, so we picked up some pizza on the way home.

We returned to the hospital after dinner and marched into Darryl's hospital room with candles on his birthday cake burning brightly. To our dismay, we learned that Darryl could not even taste his cake because of tests scheduled for the following morning. Even that didn't seem to faze him. Once again, Darryl lifted our spirits as he sat perched on his high hospital bed. A huge smile stretched across his face. I found it hard to believe that a terminal illness had attacked this alert and optimistic child. How could this bouncy bundle of energy with his active, inquisitive mind have such a short time to live? Did my reaction reveal a mother's natural inclination to deny any such possibility?

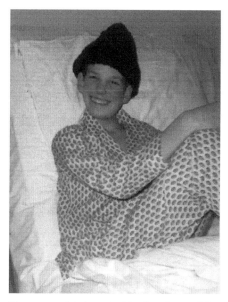

Darryl beams on his hospital bed on his 14th birthday
unfazed by his unfavorable circumstances

Several of the nurses and aides joined us as we watched Darryl blow out his candles. Together, we sang a lusty "Happy Birthday". Again, his sunny disposition captured the attention of his caregivers. Everyone had difficulty accepting the hard reality of the blow dealt to our family. Opening the picture kit, Darryl displayed his special brand of infectious joy at the thought of working on it when he returned home from the hospital. Darryl didn't complain because he couldn't eat his birthday cake. He made us all feel comfortable rather than focusing on his own problems. Although my heart continued to ache, we had a special evening as we celebrated Darryl's birthday together.

Visiting hours seemed to end early that night. We packed up the birthday cake, something of a facade since Darryl couldn't eat any of it. We also took his picture kit home because of its large size. Cautiously, we drove home respecting Denver's ice-slicked streets. The disquieting news of the day continued to overwhelm me and seemed to turn my heart as cold as that chilly, slippery street. Inside I wept. Was my son's life melting away in the same way the ice on the streets would disappear in a couple of months? As I viewed that ice-encrusted street, the depths of my being cried out, "Don't melt!"

The following afternoon, I spent considerable time with Darryl in the hospital. Having the barrage of tests behind him for another day relieved him. Harvey finished work early and would be home when the girls got out of school, so I enjoyed a nice long visit with Darryl before returning home to make supper. Harvey went to the hospital after supper. We wanted to encourage Darryl by spending as much time with him as possible. Many others visited Darryl that evening, including his piano teacher, Mrs. Orick. She brought a beautiful bouquet of flowers arranged in a vase shaped like a baseball glove.

Several friends from the Bible College where Harvey taught shared our concern and also came to visit. On the contrary, one student who often focused more on extra-curricular activities than on preparing his lessons allowed his personal agenda to carry him beyond a commiserating visit. He did bring Darryl a jigsaw puzzle as a gift, but then indicated that he wanted to speak with Harvey in the hall. He sold cemetery plots. He had learned of Darryl's prognosis and had come to make a sale determining to complete it that evening. How sad to see this young man who was pursuing a goal of becoming a pastor pervert the potential of an encouraging hospital visit.

Dollar signs clouded his vision preventing him from providing comfort to a fellow believer in difficult circumstances.

At home with the girls, I cleaned up the supper things and washed the dishes. I felt so tired and depressed. Adding to my confusion, numerous people urged us to pray for Darryl's healing. At this point, I didn't feel free to do so. I desperately wanted Darryl to live, but I knew that our loving God often sees and does things from a perspective beyond our limited understanding. From deep within, I wanted to be willing for whatever God wanted to do in Darryl's life. If that meant Darryl would become as a kernel of wheat that must physically die and be put into the ground to bring forth fruit, I wanted God's perfect plan in his life and in mine.

As I struggled, my heart cried out to God to make me willing to have a submissive spirit like Abraham. His obedience demanded that he tie his son, Isaac, on an altar in preparation to sacrifice him to God. Because Abraham demonstrated his absolute obedience, God provided a lamb and gave his beloved son back to him. Was God asking me for that same kind of loving, obedient response? And would God, in His time, bless us with a comparable restoration of our son if I walked in submission to Him?

I poured out my heart to the Lord. "Oh God, I don't know how to pray right now. I want to be willing to respond to you in the same way Abraham did when you asked him to give his son to you. Please lead me to where I should read in your Word tonight, and show me how I should pray."

Right away, I thought of Philippians 4:6-7, "Be careful for nothing; but in everything by prayer and supplication, with thanksgiving let your requests be made known unto God. And the peace of God, which passeth all understanding, shall keep your hearts and minds through Christ Jesus." As I focused on the commandments of verse 6, I cried out to God again. But this time, I also thanked Him for the peace He promised to bring to my heart. I continued to struggle with knowing how to pray about Darryl. With all my heart, I wanted to see God heal him. But did God want this for us? For Him? Would God bring glory to Himself by healing Darryl?

Earlier that day we received a letter from our daughter, Charlotte. In her letter she referenced Psalm 143 and shared that it had blessed her. I misread what she wrote and thought she said Psalm 43. So I turned to Psalm 43 and was struck by verse 5. "Why art thou cast down, O my soul? And why art thou disquieted within me? Hope in God: for I shall yet praise him, who is the health of my countenance, and my God." Next my eyes fell on Psalm 41:2-3. "The Lord will preserve him, and keep him alive . . . ," followed by, "The Lord will strengthen him upon the bed of languishing; thou wilt make all his bed in his sickness." My heart filled with hope as I concluded that God had led me to those verses. Perhaps God would bring healing to Darryl's body. Soothed by the message of those words, I continued to read God's Word and praise Him.

Still questioning, I wondered if I should share my thoughts with Harvey. I asked God to show me in some special way what to do. Harvey came home at 10:30. He smiled as he said, "Darryl was the life of the party tonight; he had so many visitors. I can't explain it, but as I left the hospital, I had a feeling that I have never had before. I felt that maybe God will heal Darryl." I considered this my sign that I could tell Harvey what had happened to me during the evening. As I told him about the verses I had read in Psalms, a settled peace encompassed me.

Throughout the week doctors ordered a variety of tests for Darryl, but a definitive diagnosis continued to elude them. These tests kept me at the hospital most afternoons and, sometimes, throughout the evenings. Because we frequently felt the need to return to the hospital together after supper, the girls became extremely tired. We decided we had to make a change. I began to limit my visits to the afternoons and Harvey arranged to spend most evenings at the hospital. This helped us to maintain a more reasonable schedule for the girls. I could then spend needed time reading, praying and talking with them at bedtime.

Somewhat frustrated by lack of results as they continued their evaluation, Darryl's doctors decided to perform abdominal surgery to obtain tissue from the lymph node in Darryl's groin. They hoped that this would provide a definitive diagnosis. They scheduled surgery for Friday night. Special friends of ours, Taylor and Jimmy Jo Gardner, picked up our girls and planned to keep them at their home for several nights. This enabled me to stay at the hospital during Darryl's surgery and recovery. It helped so much to have these friends care for them. Taylor and Jimmie Jo encouraged and helped us in many ways during those tension-filled days.

Shortly before the operation a young nurse stopped to ask, "Well Darryl, how are you doing, and how do you feel about having this operation?"

Darryl responded, "My life is in God's hands. If God takes me to heaven, I'm ready." As she left the room we saw tears in her eyes. We found out later that girls from the Bible College where Harvey taught had talked to this girl about Christ. She had responded, "I hate Jesus, and I don't want to have anything to do with the Bible or religion. I just don't like it." After her interaction with Darryl she returned to those same girls. With tears in her eyes, she told them what Darryl had said.

The hospital staff moved a teenage patient near Darryl's age into his room. In characteristic fashion, Darryl talked to him about God. They spoke about a range of subjects, including the end of the world and the expected return of Jesus. As they talked, Darryl's new friend interrupted him and with obvious great longing said, "Boy, I sure wish that I knew as much about the Bible as you do."

Harvey arrived shortly before the nurse gave Darryl an injection to get him ready for surgery. We watched as they took Darryl to the operating room. Hospital staff then moved his things to a room closer to the nurses' station to enable them to better monitor him during the night following his surgery. A friend with whom we could talk and pray, Taylor joined us in the waiting room during the operation. What a comfort.

At eight o'clock Dr. Puckett, Darryl's anesthesiologist and a personal friend from our church, came into the waiting room and told us that Darryl's operation was over. He indicated that everything had gone well.

The surgeon, Dr. Courts, also came in to tell us about the surgery. He seemed somewhat surprised by the tissue he had removed and explained, "It surely is funny looking stuff—looked much like the gland that Dr. Dragel removed a couple of weeks ago from Darryl's jaw. Oh yes," he continued, "We drained as much fluid as we could out of his left lung. Since he was lying down we could only get about half of it, about 400 cc's. I can't tell you more until Monday when they examine the tissue in the lab. We'll let you know what the lab finds."

They returned Darryl to his new room at 8:45 PM, still groggy from the anesthesia. We stayed with him until he began to sleep more restfully at about 10:30 PM. The long day and tough week had drained us both.

When we called the hospital the following morning, the nurse told us that Darryl had a good night. I hurried to get there to be with him, but he hardly recognized my presence. His pain medication made him extremely drowsy. Harvey took my place around noon. As he sat by Darryl's bedside, Dr. Courts came in and asked, "Have you ever heard of Burkitt's Disease?"

"Why yes, I have." Harvey and I had known Dr. Burkitt in Africa. In fact, he had operated on my hand in Kampala, Uganda. We had followed his research on a strain of lymphatic cancer that he discovered in Uganda. That research led him to experience success in treating this cancer with medication—a medication now being tested in the United States. Making Dr. Burkitt's research even more exciting, he had discovered an apparent link of this cancer with a virus. Our friend and mission doctor, Ted Williams, had accompanied Dr. Burkitt in his travels. They had traversed ten thousand miles of rugged central African terrain collecting the data that led to these groundbreaking discoveries. Through the careful work completed during these exploratory trips, Dr. Burkitt also discovered this particular cancer to be present only at specific altitudes, coupled with identifiable climatic conditions. Recognizing his monumental research work, his peers named this type of lymphatic cancer *Burkitt's Disease*.

Although Dr. Courts' question had generated little discussion, Darryl's sharp mind processed what he heard. As the doctor left the room, he asked Harvey, "Dad, is he talking about Burkitt's cancer?"

Harvey had to answer, "Yes," and that ended the discussion. Darryl, though very young at the time, had heard and remembered conversations in our home about Dr. Burkitt and his research.

Harvey left for home near suppertime. He told me about this conversation, adding that we needed to return to the hospital as soon as possible in case Darryl continued to struggle with more unanswered questions. We rushed through supper and, together, returned to the hospital.

Our friend Dr. Puckett stopped by. After spending a short time encouraging both Darryl and us, Dr. Puckett also asked if we had heard of Burkitt's Disease. By now, we realized that the medical professionals had been discussing the possibility that Darryl could have contracted Burkitt's Disease during our years in Africa. Darryl did not ask any more questions but remained very quiet after Dr. Puckett left. We recognized that he had not missed the implications of those questions.

As I sat beside his bed the next day, Darryl asked, "Mom would you please read the Bible to me?"

"Sure, Darryl, what do you want me to read?"

"Read the twenty-first chapter of Revelation," Darryl replied.

After I finished reading about the new heaven and the new earth and the other end-time prophesies of that chapter, he asked me to read the twenty-second chapter also. Then he exclaimed, "Oh, I just love those chapters about heaven, Mother." We had a very precious time talking about heaven.

As I opened my Bible Monday morning, I decided to read the book of James. I had forgotten about some things that James speaks of near the end of the book. I noted the opening verses of chapter 5 about being patient. I needed this admonition as I faced our uncertain future. Then, verse 15 seemed to jump off the page. It says, "The prayer offered in faith will make the sick person well; the Lord will raise him up." (NIV) Once again, my heart cried out, "Are those verses directed to me? Is that God's purpose for Darryl?"

The girls returned to school after their helpful visit to the Gardeners over the weekend. As Harvey drove me to the hospital on his way to work, we talked about the anticipated arrival of his parents from California later in the day. It would be wonderful to have their help caring for our girls since we needed to spend so much time with Darryl. Leaving me at the hospital, Harvey went on to Western while I spent the morning with Darryl. When Harvey returned, we rushed home to be present when his parents arrived shortly before noon.

Chapter 8

A DISCIPLINED LIFE FINDS STRENGTH IN GOD

*A*s we ate lunch, the ringing phone took me away from the table. When I heard Dr. Kurtz's voice, I braced myself for what would come. "Mrs. Stranske," he began, "we now have a definitive report. The lab found two strains of cancer in the tissue removed on Friday night. One of these is lymphosarcoma, a highly malignant form of cancer." Without stopping, Dr. Kurtz went on, "Children's Hospital has an oncology department that specializes in cancers found in children. A fine woman doctor, Dr. Holton, will be coming from Children's Hospital to see about admitting Darryl into their program. Recent research has produced experimental medications that show apparent success in retarding the progression of lymphosarcoma. I know that she will want to talk to you about their program. I guess that is all that I can tell you for now." I sat listening, and then thanked Dr. Kurtz.

I dropped the phone into its cradle with an uncontrolled thud then returned to the table to relay this devastating message to Harvey and his parents. As its impact engulfed us, an overwhelming pall quenched our happy conversation. Moments later Harvey said, "I think I should talk to Darryl about this tonight and tell him what the doctor told us." Harvey had received permission from Dr. Kurtz to inform Darryl about his condition as soon as we received a definitive diagnosis. He felt it important that he carry through on his commitment before others might unwittingly speak to him about it.

When the girls came home from school they greeted their grandparents with a big hug. We decided that we would all go to the hospital to visit Darryl for a short time before supper. Darryl's face lit up as his grandparents entered the room. We had a short but great visit together. While we congregated around the bed visiting with Darryl, some young people from our church came to see him. To his surprise, they gave him a gift of $100.00. The young people's group at Judson Baptist had gathered their nickels, dimes, and dollars to give to him. What a lift to receive evidence of love and concern from our church family at this agonizing time.

After supper, Harvey returned to spend time with Darryl and share with him the sad report that he did have cancer. Harvey prayed for wisdom to share the difficult information that we, with Darryl, needed to incorporate into our lives. They sat and talked for some time. Still, Harvey continued to wrestle with finding the right words to express the upsetting news.

When Harvey visited, Darryl often asked his dad to read to him from God's Word; again Darryl requested that he do so. Using the Gideon Bible on Darryl's bedside table, Harvey read from Philippians 1. Darryl listened with quiet interest until his dad read verse 12, "But I would ye should understand, brethren, that the things which happened unto me have fallen out rather unto the furtherance of the gospel . . . ."

Stopping Harvey, Darryl exclaimed, "Dad, that's just what is happening through me."

Harvey read on, "And many of the brethren in the Lord, waxing confident by my bonds, are much more bold to speak the word without fear . . . ."

Darryl interrupted again, "Just think, Dad, kids at church and kids at school are getting to know about God because of me. They're getting to know that God is working in my life."

As Harvey continued to read, Darryl's eyes sparkled, and he couldn't wait for his dad to finish reading verses 20 and 21, "According to my earnest expectation and my hope, that in nothing I shall be ashamed, but that with all boldness, as always, so now also Christ shall be magnified in my body, whether it be by life or by death. For to me to live is Christ, and to die is gain."

"That's it, Dad! That's exactly what I feel and believe. Would you print those verses out on a piece of paper and put them on my tray so anyone coming in here can see them?"

Harvey complied with his request while quietly praying for wisdom for the words he still needed to speak. After Harvey printed the requested portions of Philippians 1:12-14, 20-21 in large letters to Darryl's satisfaction, he gave it to Darryl who placed it on his meal tray so that anyone coming to his bedside could not miss seeing his proclamation:

> But I would ye should understand, brethren, that the things which happened unto me have fallen out rather unto the furtherance of the gospel . . . And many of the brethren in the Lord, waxing confident by my bonds, are much more bold to speak the word without fear.
>
> According to my earnest expectation and my hope, that in nothing I shall be ashamed, but that with all boldness, as always, so now also Christ shall be magnified in my body, whether it be by life, or by death.
>
> For to me to live is Christ, and to die is gain.

Then, in a quiet voice, Harvey expressed, "Darryl, you really mean those last words that I wrote down for you, don't you?"

"Oh, yes, Dad, I really do. I'd love to go and see Jesus."

Sobered by Darryl's words, Harvey paused briefly and then continued, "You know, Darryl, you may be experiencing that next step in 'life' very soon. Dr. Kurtz called this afternoon to tell us that they have definitely found cancer."

Without hesitation, Darryl responded, "You know, Dad, I had sort of figured that out because of your conversation with the doctors about Burkitt's Disease. Can they cure it?"

Reaching out and putting his hand on Darryl's arm, Harvey replied, "They don't give us much hope of a cure, Darryl, but a doctor from Children's Hospital wants to come and evaluate your situation. They have experimental drugs that have helped some children with this kind of cancer. They feel that these drugs might at least slow down the progress of your cancer."

Quiet for a short time Darryl responded, "Dad, if God has planned it this way, then it is the very best for me. And if it is the best for me, then it must be the best for you and Mom too."

"Yes, Darryl, but we must not forget that God can still perform miracles no matter how impossible the situation looks. If it would bring Him greater glory, God can heal you."

"But Dad," Darryl persevered, "maybe that wouldn't be best." Darryl remained silent for a long time, both he and his dad lost in their own thoughts. Then Darryl asked, "Before you go, Dad, would you read the twenty-third Psalm?"

"Sure, Darryl, I'd love to."

Harvey had barely finished reading that beloved portion of God's Word before Darryl exclaimed, "Just think, Dad, I'm walking in the valley of the shadow of death and I'm not afraid. Dad, would you add that verse in Psalms 23 to the other verses you printed out? I mean the verse that talks about going through the valley of death and not being afraid." Responding to Darryl's request, Harvey added the words of Psalms 23:4 to the other verses on Darryl's declaration of trust, "Yea, though I walk through the valley of the shadow of death, I will fear no evil: for thou art with me; thy rod and thy staff they comfort me."

Having complied with Darryl's latest request, Harvey and Darryl shared a deep silence for some time, thinking of the weighty matters which they had discussed. It was getting late and Darryl needed to sleep. Harvey, too, needed sleep so that he could teach his classes in the morning. It was difficult for Harvey to leave but God gave grace for the heaviness of his father-heart as Darryl and he prayed together committing future days and events into God's almighty and loving hands.

While Harvey visited Darryl that evening, I read the next story in their Bible story book to our girls—the story of Jesus healing the nobleman's son. Jesus made a promise to the concerned father, and the man believed what Jesus told him. Upon returning home he found his son healed of his illness. Furthermore, it had happened at the same time that the man had pled with Jesus to heal him. Again, I wondered, will God work a similar miracle for Darryl? Or, what did God have in His plan for Darryl?

Darryl had wanted to include a tract with the Christmas card he gave to his customers before Christmas. He asked his dad to help him find a good one that would tell his customers why Jesus had come to this earth. He thought of doing this too close to Christmas so they could not find enough copies of any tract that communicated what Darryl wanted to say. Harvey applauded him for his desire and suggested that he delay his plan until next year. Harvey assured him that we would plan earlier, enabling him to obtain what he wanted before supplies sold out.

Now, Darryl's situation changed but we remembered that he wanted to share his love for Jesus with his customers. Recognizing this, we decided that God had given another opportunity to fulfill Darryl's desire while, at the same time, letting his customers know why Darryl had to give up his route. We would write a letter to his customers.

Darryl had retained control of his paper route from his hospital bed. His friend, Butch, who lived next door to us subbed for him and kept him informed about his route by phone. But with the serious nature of Darryl's illness confirmed, we recognized that he had to relinquish control of his route. We felt that Darryl's serene acceptance of his life-threatening illness spoke volumes about his sincere trust in his Heavenly Father; we wanted to communicate this, too, in our proposed letter.

That attitude remained as I spent time with Darryl the next morning. Our pastor came to visit and Darryl responded to his greeting by informing him that he had cancer yet expressing his trust in God's sovereignty. When nurses came to care for him, they routinely asked him how he felt. As he had told our pastor, he would assure them, "I'm doing okay because I'm in God's hands." Hearing him speak with such confidence caused me to think again that Darryl showed maturity far beyond his fourteen years.

Before leaving, I shared our idea about sending out a letter to his paper route customers. I explained that this would allow us to let them know why he no longer delivered their papers along with providing an opportunity to share his love for Jesus as he had wanted to do before Christmas. Darryl concurred with our suggestion with great enthusiasm.

Later in the day, Harvey interacted further with Darryl about the content of the proposed letter. He also suggested that we talk to Butch about including the letter as he folded papers for delivery. Butch agreed to our proposal. Speaking to him about the letter opened the door for Harvey to have an extended conversation with him. Butch began to ask questions about Darryl and about the letter we planned to write. They talked for more than an hour and Harvey explained the way of salvation to him. Butch seemed close to making a decision to trust Christ as Savior, but delayed life's most important choice, saying, "I've never heard anything like this before. I have to think about it."[3]

While I visited with Darryl that afternoon, Dr. Dragel came into the room. He was the surgeon who had removed the diseased gland in Darryl's jaw before Christmas. After talking for a few minutes he motioned for me to come out into the hall to talk to him. There he said, "Well Mrs. Stranske, I guess you know what is going on by now."

"Yes, and Darryl does too."

---

[3] An explanation of how to make life's most important decision is found in Appendix I

With a note of near dismay in his voice he asked, "He does? And what does he say?"

"As soon as he heard about it, he told us that if this is what God has for him, this is the very best thing that could be happening."

Dr. Dragel looked at me with complete shock. Looking down at the floor, he stood in total silence for several moments. Shaking his head in disbelief, he seemed to struggle to get the words out, "I've had old people that don't take this kind of news without falling apart." Other doctors who had shared either in consultation about or diagnosis of Darryl's condition also expressed astonishment as Dr. Dragel spread the word of his response. A young boy accepting this devastating diagnosis with such calmness and equanimity amazed them.

Late that afternoon Harvey and I completed work on the letter that we wanted to send to Darryl's customers. We worked and reworked its content with further input from Darryl until we agreed on what needed to be said:

Dear Neighbor,

Our son, Darryl, has been your Rocky Mountain News boy during the past few months. We have just been told that Darryl has a highly malignant type of cancer. The doctors feel that there is no medicine which can cure this and that Darryl has only a short time to live.

Although many of you have not been aware of it, Darryl has had a greater interest in you than just being able to provide you with the Rocky Mountain News. He has been praying for some time that he could effectively share with each one of you his love for the Lord Jesus Christ. He wanted to do this because he wanted you, his customer, to know that you are prepared to meet God. Darryl has found such real joy in experiencing this himself that he has constantly tried to share what he knows with his friends. He has done this at school and has wanted to share with you too.

Darryl will be receiving some treatment for his disease. Therefore, the doctor felt it best that I tell him what has been found. The reality of Darryl's confidence in God came through strong as he asked me, his Dad, to write out several verses of scripture so that he could put them beside his hospital bed where all of his visitors could see them. The verses that he said that he wanted to claim for his own and that he asked me to write are:

But I would ye should understand, brethren, that the things which happened to me have fallen out rather unto the furtherance of the gospel . . . . and many of the brethren in the Lord, waxing confident by my bonds, are much more bold to speak the word without fear . . . .

According to my earnest expectation and my hope, that in nothing I shall be ashamed, but that with all boldness, as always, so now also Christ shall be magnified in my body, whether it be by life, or by death.

FOR TO ME TO LIVE IS CHRIST,
AND TO DIE IS GAIN.
(Philippians 1:12, 14, 20-21)

Darryl told me, "Dad that is exactly what I feel and believe and I want everyone to know it."

As I talked to him about the implications of the disease in his body, I asked him if it made him afraid, to which he replied, "No . . . , no . . . Dad, but it just makes me sad to think that P—F—(a school friend) doesn't know the Lord Jesus yet, and so he isn't ready to die. But I know that he will come to know the Lord Jesus, because I've been praying for him."

Before I left the hospital, Darryl asked me to read one more thing for him. He wanted me to read the 23rd Psalm. After I read it, Darryl turned to me with a smile on his face and said, "Just think, Dad, I'm walking in the valley of the shadow of death, and, Dad, I'm not afraid because God is with me."

Why do I share all of this with you? First, because Darryl would want me to do it; and then, because Darryl has found reality. His mother and I share that same reality which gives us peace of heart at the same time that our mother—and father—hearts cry out to keep Darryl with us and see him grow into manhood.

Further, we would love to share with you how you also can have peace in your heart such as we know. The Lord Jesus Christ died on the cross, paying the penalty for your sin and for our sin by His shed blood. By accepting this provision which God has made to cleanse and purify us from sin, we can experience peace with God and freedom from fear—even in the face of death.

The doctor tells us that Darryl will be in Porter Hospital for a few more days; then will probably be at home with us for a time. He would love to see or hear from some of you, and I am sure, as he would have strength, he would love to share, personally, his faith in Jesus Christ.

Or, if our sharing this with you has aroused a desire in any of you to know more about how you could experience this peace with God, please let us know. Darryl's mother and/or I would love to take time to show you from the Bible, God's Word, how you also can experience this life that God has provided for us in the Lord Jesus Christ.

Because we are interested in you,
Harvey and Evadene Stranske

PS: Although the doctors have told us that there is no known cure for Darryl's disease, our God is still able and does perform miracles. For those of Darryl's customers who are children of God and so can pray, we would appreciate it if you would pray with us that God's perfect will might be done in Darryl's body. If God still has work for Darryl to do, He is able even to perform a miracle in Darryl's body. We do not ask for this unless God could be glorified through it. We agree with Darryl that we want Christ to "be magnified . . . whether it be by life, or by death."

After Harvey typed and copied this letter, Butch included a copy into each early morning paper. The response overwhelmed us. As usual, I had gone to the hospital as early as possible to be with Darryl, and Harvey had rushed off to his office. Telephone calls inundated Harvey's mother who still visited us. Children of parents on Darryl's route took the letter to school. Someone from school called and asked for permission to use part of the letter in their school paper. As soon as school dismissed that afternoon, an amazing number of Darryl's classmates at Dunstan Junior High called him at the hospital.

Hearing the diagnosis of Darryl's illness through the letter, Peter, the special friend alluded to in the letter, couldn't restrain his tears as he called. I heard Darryl comforting him. He assured him that he would be all right and told Peter not to worry about him.

That afternoon, a girl from one of Darryl's classes came to the hospital. Harvey had arrived from work a few minutes before to free me to go home for a bit. This young friend of Darryl's, however, appeared so distraught and in tears that we knew we had to try to help her. While Darryl slept, we took her into a nearby room so we could talk. She searched for a way to communicate, unable to speak through her tears. Without saying why, she handed Harvey a comic book. Turning to me, she handed me a big sucker. We assumed that she wanted us to give these to Darryl. Then, through her tears she blurted out, "It's not fair! It's just not fair! Darryl is one of the nicest kids in school."

I tried to soothe her. Seeing that Darryl's life had made a deep impression on her, I tried to help her understand how Darryl looked at his life in this critical time. She listened intently as I explained that the time that we, as humans, have here on earth is only a speck of time compared to eternity, even for a person who lives a long life. God has created us as eternal beings, and Darryl looked forward to spending all of eternity in heaven. Recognizing this, Darryl wanted to live whatever time he had on earth in a way that would bring glory to God.

I then went on to explain how she, too, could experience the same peace that Darryl exhibited by believing in the Lord Jesus Christ as her Savior. I shared with our troubled new friend that we do not have to worry about whether things are fair or not. God always does what is best for us. From our human perspective, we may not understand the hurt and grief that engulfs us, but we find comfort in the fact that God loves us and works out his eternal purpose in us and through us. I don't know her total reaction to our conversation, but she seemed less agitated as she left.

We continued to look in awe as we observed the impact Darryl's response to his illness had on others. As Darryl's anesthesiologist, Dr. Hoffer, visited that evening, he spoke of the stark contrast between Darryl's response and that of patients who did not know God. He had just come from visiting such a patient, an older man without hope and unable to cope. Marveling at Darryl's outlook and concern for others rather than himself, Dr. Hoffer talked about the difficulty of dealing with people with critical illnesses who have no faith. He told us that the perspective between Darryl and this hurting man contrasted beyond belief.

Doctor Hoffer's son, a friend of Darryl's from church, also came to visit. Darryl beamed with excitement as his friend shared how Darryl's response to his illness had produced a profound affect in his life. Seeing Darryl speak up for his Lord had led him to make a new commitment to live for Christ and do whatever God wanted him to do.

As Harvey and I walked out of the room with Dr. Hoffer, he spoke again about the seriousness of Darryl's illness and the hopelessness of his situation from a human standpoint. He then added, "As doctors, we never say always, and don't ever say never." This small spark of hope, coming from our godly doctor friend encouraged us to think that God might yet spare our son.

Dr. Holton from Children's Hospital had come to see Darryl during the day. After examining and talking to him, she believed that Darryl seemed to be a good candidate for the experimental treatment available at Children's Hospital. She recommended that he move to Children's Hospital as soon as possible to begin treatment. We expressed concern because we did not want to subject Darryl to useless, added suffering. Would these experimental drugs really provide relief and healing? After struggling with these questions, we gave our permission for this treatment. They moved him the following morning at around 8:30, and a whole new set of doctors began a series of tests in preparation for the chemotherapy treatment planned for him.

Although it seemed as if life had already dealt us more than our share of physical and emotional ups and downs, we discovered more ahead. After we arrived home, Harvey received a call from the Rocky Mountain News. The aggravated caller asked, "What are you doing anyway? Our switchboard has lighted up like a Christmas tree all day because of a letter you had inserted in the paper today. Are you trying to get money or something?"

Surprised by this intimation, Harvey tried to reassure him, "Why no, we never thought of anything like that. We don't want money. We have adequate insurance which covers Darryl's hospital bills." Then Harvey added, "You know, you need to read the letter we had included with the paper before insinuating that we're after money."

Quieting down, the gruff sounding caller stated, "Well we felt we needed to check and see what you had to say."

We later found that people on Darryl's paper route had shared our letter with their friends all over the Denver area. Wanting to get further information, these people had joined Darryl's customers in calling the Rocky Mountain News. Some even suggested—or demanded—that this letter be printed in the paper. We could understand why this caused some consternation in the editorial offices.

We realized with amazement that something beyond human explanation was transpiring. It was a God-thing! We saw Him answer specific prayers. For some time, I felt deep concern for some of our neighbors and had asked God for a way in which we could tell them about the love of the Lord Jesus.

In a different way than I anticipated, God opened the door for sharing that message through the letter we sent because of Darryl's illness.

Darryl had also asked God for opportunities to share his love for the Lord Jesus with schoolmates as well as with his paper route customers. Now God had provided the means for Darryl to get their responsive attention. Additionally, we felt concern for the young people of our church and we had prayed that God would make them more tender toward the things of God. A number of young people expressed a commitment to make some definite changes in the direction of their lives. Yes, our hearts ached, but we thanked God for what we saw Him doing.

Chapter 9

NEW MEDICATIONS PROVIDE HOPE

hildren's Hospital in Denver admitted Darryl ten days after his birthday. While hospital staff began their entry examination process, Dr. Holton took us into her office. Seating us across from her desk, she addressed us in her straightforward manner, "I'd like to share the procedures with you that Darryl faces. Our staff will give him a blood test, x-rays, a spinal tap, and take a bone marrow sample this morning. To obtain the bone marrow sample, we must insert a large needle into his hip. Although impossible to eliminate pain, we feel we do this in a better and less hurtful way than most."

"Why do you need a bone marrow sample?"

"By this we can tell if his cancer has moved into the bone marrow. If it has, Darryl's cancer will have progressed to the leukemia stage. In time, lymphosarcoma often enters the bone marrow and becomes leukemia also. We will begin chemotherapy after we complete these tests. We hope that the powerful medications included in his chemotherapy treatment will move him into remission."

"Does this usually happen?"

Dr. Holton hesitated and then replied, "It does most of the time, but not always." She continued, "Although Darryl's illness is considered terminal, I still have hope. I always wait for my phone to ring, telling me that a new and more powerful drug has been found that will cure these diseases. So, don't lose hope."

"Will he be in the hospital long," I queried, "and what can we expect if he goes into remission?"

"We expect him to respond to the chemotherapy, and if he does, we believe that he will be back in school in a couple of weeks. If his body responds like we hope and he goes into remission, he may have several good months where he will feel close to normal. He will be in the hospital now for a few days, and then we will continue to treat him on an outpatient basis."

Shocked by what she said, we wondered if we heard correctly. After all, Dr. Kurtz felt quite certain that Darryl would only live for a month or two, at the most. We didn't expect that he would ever return to school. Of course, Dr. Kurtz had shared his assessment with us before he knew that Darryl might enter this experimental program.

Dr. Holton's next words did not sound quite so encouraging. "Darryl's age is against him. Puberty is the worst time to obtain a continuing response to the treatment of this disease. Because a teenager's body matures at a rapid pace, cancer cells also multiply rapidly. In Darryl's favor, we are accumulating increasing evidence that, in ways we do not understand, an individual's mental outlook may affect the growth of cancer cells; therefore, Darryl's positive attitude toward life could impact the outcome."

Dr. Holton added, "I think I should tell you that we are having a medical conference—in progress right now—with doctors from many places. They are discussing cases just like, or similar to, Darryl's. One of the participating doctors is recognized for his expertise in this particular field. Because of the focus of the conference, these doctors plan to examine Darryl, after which they will discuss his case in depth. Do you have any questions?"

We had taken in more information than our tired minds could comprehend or assimilate. I could only answer, "No, I guess not; not now anyhow."

We left Dr. Holton's office with mixed feelings. On one hand we felt devastated, realizing with renewed force the horrendous foe we faced. Darryl had such a fierce fire burning in his young body; could anything or anyone reverse this devastating intruder? On the other hand, we had some hope. Research continued and medical science experienced some progress. Could one of these new drugs extinguish such a fire?

We sat in the waiting room throughout the morning deep in thought. After completing all of the necessary procedures, they rolled Darryl back into his hospital room. One of the doctors informed us that Darryl had received the first of his medications and described it as "a jolt of super strong stuff." This included vincristine, cytoxan and allopurinol by injection, as well as prednisone by mouth. Again we struggled with that ongoing nagging but hopeful question, "Would God use modern science and developing knowledge of this dread disease and its treatment to restore life and health to our son?"

We left Darryl as noon approached. Harvey returned in the evening and found him in good spirits. The next morning I called Children's Hospital to inquire about him. To my surprise, they said, "Darryl did great and didn't even get sick from the medicine. You can come in and take him home."

Stunned and almost unbelieving, I replied, "That's wonderful. We'll come right over to get him."

Harvey went to the hospital to bring Darryl home while his parents and I made some quick changes to prepare the house for Darryl's return. Harvey's parents had been staying in Darryl's basement bedroom. We decided that they should stay there, and we prepared an upstairs room for him that would be closer to our bedroom. Since Faith slept in a double bed, we moved Susan in with Faith, leaving Susan's room for Darryl. By the time Harvey and Darryl arrived home, we had things ready.

As Harvey left the hospital, the staff reminded him again that we needed to restrict visitors when Darryl returned home. His left lung, from which they had drained a large quantity of fluid during his operation only a week before, had again filled with fluid. He needed shielding from exposure to any illness that would impact his lungs. Not wanting to jeopardize Darryl's recovery, we carefully enforced this rule.

We did make one exception. Peter called when he heard of Darryl's release from the hospital. Pleading, he said that he had to see Darryl. Darryl also anxiously wanted to see Peter. We knew that God had been speaking to him, and that Peter wrestled with some of the things Darryl had said to him. Not wanting to hinder something that God might want to do in Peter's life, we agreed to let him come over for a short time. Their animated conversation reflected the depth of their friendship. Then, in the midst of that conversation, Peter blurted out, "Darryl, if God heals you, then I'll believe."

Without missing a beat, Darryl retorted, "Peter you may not see God heal me, and you may not even see me die, because Jesus said that he will come back again and He may return before either of those things happen. But Peter, Jesus wants you to be ready to meet God."

Peter seemed so close to committing his life to Christ that day; but to Darryl's continuing sorrow and concern, he again delayed making that important decision. We didn't let Darryl have any other visitors but he received numerous phone calls from friends. One schoolmate especially encouraged Darryl by telling him that God had been speaking to him through Darryl's response to his illness. He was now convinced that God was calling him to become a minister.

Dr. Holton called us on Sunday to tell us that Darryl's bone marrow report came back all clear. This reassuring good news encouraged us. That same afternoon we received an unexpected call from someone at Biola College. They reported that a number of students at Biola felt deeply concerned when they heard about Darryl. Setting up a fund, generous Biola students—many struggling to meet their own school bills—donated sufficient money to send Charlotte, Ray and Tim home for a visit because of Darryl's illness. They wanted to make sure these three siblings saw their brother one last time in case he died soon. What a special and loving gift those students provided for each of us, but especially for Darryl. Tim's schedule allowed him to leave before Charlotte and Ray, so he arrived home the following Tuesday. Since we had decided not to tell Darryl about this anticipated visit, his face registered surprise beyond description when Tim walked into his room. Then learning that Char and Ray had also received tickets to come home, he could hardly wait.

Chapter 10

ROCKY MOUNTAIN NEWS STORY GENERATES PHONE AND MAIL STORM

On Wednesday we received another surprise call from the Rocky Mountain News—six days after the first call. This time, a cordial voice greeted Harvey. Identifying himself, the caller asked, "Could we do a story on your son, Darryl?"

Taken aback, Harvey replied, "Well, yes, I guess that would be all right."

Reflecting the persistence of a reporter, he next asked, "Would it be all right if a photographer and I came out right now and had an interview with Darryl?"

Although late in the day, Harvey responded, "I think that would work out—if Darryl feels up to it and agrees."

Harvey reported Darryl's consent to his caller who replied, "We'll be right over."

Soon the reporter and his photographer sat in our living room. Their huge camera set up toward one corner of the sitting area seemed overpowering. Although our visitors showed consideration in their interaction with Darryl, we felt concern for him in his weakened condition as the reporter pressed him to reveal his "real" feelings about his illness. In trying to understand an attitude foreign to him, the reporter questioned Darryl in diverse ways about his reaction to the sentence of death hanging over him.

Each time Darryl responded with quiet assurance that death held no fear for him; he looked forward to his new home in heaven with Jesus when he died. As the interview continued, Darryl answered each question with calmness and the joy of Christ radiating from his face. Glancing at the photographer sitting across the room with his camera, both Harvey and I saw tears welling up in his eyes and, sometimes, even trickling down his face.

After the reporter completed his interview and the photographer had taken several pictures, they gathered their paraphernalia to leave. Harvey stopped the reporter at the door, "I do have one request to make of you. If you should use this story, I beg you to please honestly report the things Darryl has told you and not change his words or their meaning in any way."

"I'll try to do my best on that."

That night we asked the people at our regular mid-week evening prayer service at church to pray with us about the story that might develop from the interview. We requested they pray for an accurate report of the words and message that Darryl shared with the reporter. We further asked them to pray that the words printed would communicate a strong witness for Christ.

On Thursday, we went to the airport to pick up Char and Ray. As we made our way home, our college kids began singing a chorus that we hadn't heard before. What a comforting message the words of this song conveyed:

> I've got confidence
> God is going to see me through
> No matter what the case may be
> I know he's going to fix it for me.[4]

Although our children didn't know it, I laid beneath an additional cloud. On a recent visit, one of the doctors at the oncology clinic had suggested the

---

[4] "I've Got Confidence" by Andrae' Crouch. Copyright © 1969 Bud John Songs (ASCAP) (adm. at EM!CMGPublishing.com) All rights reserved. Used by permission. International Copyright Secured. All Rights Reserved. Used by Permission.

possibility that our older children could also have glandular problems with potential involvement similar to Darryl's. The drumbeat of their words kept running through my mind causing me to wonder how I could bear having others in our family also in jeopardy. The chorus our kids sang spoke to me right where I needed help. Our Heavenly Father knew all about our struggles—my struggles. He had not lost control of our lives. He would see us through whatever difficult days might lie ahead. I needed to put my trust in God and rest in Him.

Doctors at the oncology clinic requested that we bring our three older children to the clinic to be examined. Consequently, Charlotte, Ray and Tim accompanied Darryl to his Friday appointment. Thankfully, their examination revealed no detectable related problems.

Meanwhile, we checked the Rocky Mountain News on Thursday morning for Darryl's story. Nothing. Then Friday morning; again, nothing. When the story did not appear on Saturday morning, I concluded that the editors had decided not to use it.

On Saturday evening, we received an excited call from a friend. He could hardly contain himself as he exclaimed, "Have you seen the Sunday paper that came out tonight?"

"No, why do you ask?"

"Well, you ought to see it. There's a big article about Darryl with a picture of him holding his violin; and it's right on the front page."

"You must be kidding," I almost shouted.

"No, I'm not kidding—and the article is just great."

Through my excitement I managed to tell my friend, "Thank you so much for letting us know."

Harvey rushed out and bought several copies of the Rocky Mountain News because we knew we would want extra copies to clip and send to family and friends. When he returned, Harvey brought the papers he had purchased to the basement recreation room. We all sat on the camp cots set up to provide a place for our college tribe to sleep since we currently had a very full house. The student body at Western Bible Institute had grown, resulting in insufficient dorm space. With our older kids away at school, we had offered room and board to two male students. They had returned to their basement room following Christmas break. So, in addition to these two Western students, we now temporarily housed our three visiting college kids and Harvey's parents who had come to help us and still remained.

After scanning the lengthy article, Harvey said, "This is absolutely amazing! They got it straight."[5] We marveled as we read the story; God had again answered our prayers in an exciting way. We sensed that this positive story would bring glory to our Lord. Flooded with gratitude, we stopped to thank God for it and ask Him to impact many readers by the message presented. We then called our pastor and told him how God had answered our prayer and the prayers of God's people at church concerning the article. Even then, we wondered if the Five Star Edition published on Sunday morning might cut the story or put it in a less prominent place. But no! It still adorned the front page. We learned that, because of Darryl's story, the Rocky Mountain News sold out throughout the Denver area; in fact, no copies could be found by noon. Darryl expressed delight and excitement. Because of his illness and through this article, he received the opportunity to witness to people throughout the Denver area and beyond. Darryl couldn't sleep, but felt the need to return a letter to his cousin, Connie, in California. Earlier she had written, "I just decided to write to tell you what a comfort you have been to me. If you can be cheerful even on the last trial God puts you through, I have no right to complain about earthly problems . . . ." Darryl then penned a letter to Connie after his story appeared in the paper; much later a member of the family sent us a copy of that letter. In it, Darryl had written:

Dear Connie,

Can you believe what God's doing? If you saw the clippings I sent you [he had enclosed a copy of the news article], just think

---

[5]   The full text of the Rocky Mountain News article appears in Appendix II

of what a witness that's going to be to all the people around here! Isn't it wonderful the way that they didn't get things (especially spiritual) mixed up the way newspapers have a way of doing? You can just see God's hand in all of this. It's just been hard to believe all the channels of witness God has opened up! It is just so wonderful to see how God can really use us as a tool in His hand. God has to, and is going to, take all of the credit for this. After all, what did I have to do with getting myself sick (a real blessing in disguise!)? God is totally in control of everything that has happened to me! I can't do anything but praise God for everything He's done, "and the supply of the spirit of Jesus Christ . . . . (For) Christ shall be magnified in my body, whether it be by life or death. For to me to live is Christ and to die is gain! . . . I am in a straight betwixt two, having a desire to depart, and to be with Christ; which is far better: Nevertheless to abide in the flesh is more needful for you" (see Philippians 1:19-24), because God is going to do what He knows is best in my life! "For it is God which worketh in you both to will and to do of HIS good pleasure" (Phil. 2:13).

Connie, I'm just all bubbling up with joy! I feel like I could sit down and write those words right along with Paul. It makes me feel wonderful that God can use me as a tool even in your life!

I need badly to tell you of at least a portion of what God has done so far. I was able to talk to a boy today who at first told me he questioned his salvation because he hadn't seen reality in his own life. He's saved, both he and I found out, all he needed to do was just turn his whole life over to God. He went away with an assurance of salvation and if God keeps working in him, a new dedicated life!

Another friend of mine, one who I've been praying for three years, is coming over to make a decision for Christ this week! A $250 Faith Promise God has faithfully given through gifts from friends at school. This is the first faith-promise God has directed me to give like this. I had no idea where it was coming from a year ago when I made it. [Note: Darryl had not received this gift at this time, nor did he know how much it would be. A friend told him that students were gathering funds for him at school.]

I could go on and on and on etc. 'til you would get tired of reading my scribbled handwriting of all God's working. Now I better just say, "PRAISE THE LORD!!!"

I'm getting along fine right now. I may get to go back to school a week from Monday. According to their first analysis I was supposed to be gone from this earth by then! What a strange feeling to be living on time that just seems to be borrowed. I have no idea how long God is going to keep me on this earth. But be it long or be it short, God's in control of it all! HIS will is what's going to be best to glorify His name! Write soon!

> To a sister in our wonderful Savior, Jesus Christ,
> Darryl

In response to this letter, Connie wrote:

Guess what! We had a mother's meeting at our house (it was a church group). The assistant pastor's wife saw the letter that you wrote me and my mom let them read it. She said, everybody was sniveling over it. But listen, the assistant pastor's wife said that it should be given to the pastor and have him read it from the pulpit! How does that grab you? Next Sunday he will read it.

Written later:

Today is Sunday and I just have to tell you what happened. The pastor told the people about you and then he read the letter. Everyone was crying. It was so neat, you are such a good example. Nobody could believe you are only 14 because your faith is so firm . . . . The letter is going to be mimeographed and sent out because so many people want it. All I can say is PRAISE THE LORD!

As people read the Sunday edition of the Rocky Mountain News our telephone kept ringing and ringing. In one call an excited teenage boy told Harvey about their morning church service. "You know we haven't had anyone saved in our church for several years," he began. "Then today, our pastor got up to preach and told us, 'I prepared a message for this morning, but I'm putting it aside. I'm just going to read part of the Rocky Mountain News to you.'" With that as an introduction, he read the whole article about Darryl from the paper. Then, when he asked people to respond to Christ, fourteen young people came forward to accept Christ.

Harvey thanked the young caller for sharing this encouraging news with him and added, "Praise God."

One of Harvey's students called from Evergreen, a nearby community. With her voice choking up, she had a hard time speaking. Gaining control, she told Harvey about her next-door neighbor. She had been praying for this neighbor and trying to tell her about God's free gift of salvation. The neighbor had let her know that she did not want to be bothered with that kind of talk but continued to accept her friendship. On this Sunday morning, however, before our friend got out of bed, she heard an insistent knock on her door. Opening the door, she found her skeptic neighbor with a copy of the Rocky Mountain News in her hands. "Can you believe this?" she shouted. "Just listen to what it says!"

She had not read far before our friend stopped her; now she really could not believe what she heard. "You know that's about my teacher at school and his son who has cancer." Her neighbor completed reading the entire article to her and then they continued talking over a cup of coffee. When this neighbor who had been so resistant to any mention of God returned home, she left as a newborn child of God.

We had other kinds of responses too. Some well-meaning people insisted that we try some new cancer treatment. A number of callers urged us to seek healing from Catherine Kuhlman or Oral Roberts. One man called, assuring us that he had some special psychic power and wanted to cure our son. I felt surrounded by an evil presence. When I told him that we trusted Jesus in this situation, he became enraged. Yelling into the phone, he told me that we didn't love our son. If we loved him, we would let our caller come over, and he would heal Darryl right that day. Shaken, I terminated our conversation as quickly as possible.

Soon letters filled our mailbox addressed to both Darryl and to us. On more than one day, our mailbox could not contain all the letters received. The United Press had reprinted a condensed version of the story across the country. Although they shortened the text, they included the picture of Darryl with his violin and printed it all over the United States and beyond; we heard from people in twenty-three states, the District of Columbia and three foreign countries. Some letters came in care of our church in Denver, because it had been mentioned in the article. One letter reached us simply addressed, "To the Boy Who's Not Afraid to Die, Denver, Colorado." We lived in the city of Lakewood, adjacent to Denver; however, the post office delivered it to our home since the picture on the front page of the paper had shown Darryl holding his violin with the caption, "He's not afraid to die."

One letter came from Mrs. Schictell in New Jersey. She read the article in her hometown paper. Several years before, she had lived in the wealthy Willowbrook area across the road from the campus of Western Bible Institute. In fact, we had carpooled together when her son and our daughter, Faith, attended kindergarten. Seeing the article in her New Jersey paper, she called an old neighbor of hers to verify if this could possibly be the same Darryl Stranske she had known. The two women spent time reminiscing about things they remembered Darryl had said and done. Mrs. Schictell got our address from her friend and told us about their conversation when she wrote. She also sent a very nice labyrinth game made out of wood for Darryl, a game which she said her family had enjoyed and found challenging.

Surprisingly, Darryl's story even penetrated the White House. To his delight, Darryl received a personal letter from President Nixon in which the president said:

> A news item about you and your many accomplishments came to my attention recently. You have shown great courage in the face of your illness, and your strength is a remarkable example to others. It is clear that you believe, as I do, that faith does perform miracles, and I hope this faith will sustain you in the future. With best wishes,
>
> Sincerely,
Richard Nixon

Later in the week, Harvey received a call from a man in Chicago. He told Harvey that he had read the story about our son in the Chicago paper. He had a hard time believing that a fourteen-year old boy could take the news of his impending death so well. Harvey responded, "Yes, it is unusual, but it grows out of his deep and real faith in God."

The man then told Harvey that he called because he also had a son suffering with terminal cancer. His son had become angry and fought against his disease. This concerned father wanted to know if Harvey could tell him how to help his son accept his illness. Harvey attempted to explain Darryl's quiet acceptance of his disease. He shared with this troubled father that Darryl had such deep inner peace because he knew that he belonged to God and that, even if he died, God would take him to heaven. Darryl felt secure in relying on his Heavenly Father who works everything together for good for those who love Him. Because of this, he could accept with equanimity such a negative diagnosis. As this hurting father listened attentively and asked questions, Harvey explained God's wonderful gift of salvation to him. This new friend thanked him for his help and Harvey assured him that we would pray for his son, and for him. Harvey received a similar call from someone in Iowa, and again had the privilege of sharing this wonderful message with a woman who hurt for her son who could not willingly accept his illness.

Darryl's life and his response to his illness touched an ever-widening circle of people all over the country. At the same time, his attitude affected his siblings—and our whole family. Following Christmas vacation, Ray wrote Darryl: "God has really taught me a lot, Darryl, through the things you shared from God's Word while we were home and just seeing your attitude in this hard time." Later, Ray wrote again, "This is a card for a super brother. Thanks so much for the encouragement you've been to me. I'm praying for you Darryl and I know God is going to use you to really glorify Him."

Charlotte wrote, "Darryl, you've been such a sweet example of the Life of Christ—a fragrance unto life—to me this past year, and I praise God for the way He's used you in my life to stimulate me to trust more in our Lord. I've grown to love you very much . . ."

In a letter signed, "Tim (Your rival sibling)," Tim asked Darryl to read Psalm 103, then continued by saying,

> That [Psalm] really meant a lot to me, so I thought I'd share it with you. A lot of kids in my Sunday School class are praying for you, and all kinds of people have been asking about you at Biola . . . . I just thank God for the testimony you have been to us and to so many others. God works in the lives of young people and His grace is sufficient for all our needs. I love you lots.

Darryl's life and witness had earlier impacted another relative who lived in Washington. My niece, Glenelle, wrote,

> Evadene, when my mother first wrote of Darryl's illness my first reaction was a mother's disbelieving grief and horror. Randy [her son] gave me the dearest smile and said "You know, Mom, Darryl's such a great guy. God must have a special chore for him. The Lord knows what we surely can't."

Darryl had introduced Randy to Christ two years earlier while we visited my sister (Randy's Grandmother) in San Jose, California.

Noting the difference in life and outlook produced by the diverse foundations laid in two young lives, a letter from Denver compared Darryl's story to another article published in a recent Rocky Mountain News,

> I couldn't help compare Darryl's story with so many accounts of other teenagers, particularly the story that was publicized not long ago about a 17 year-old young man that committed suicide because he was hung up on drugs and felt there was no other way out. His story was sad and futile, where-as Darryl's story is heart breaking, yet in a sense beautiful as it shows forth the glory of God in his life.

> How many other people saw the distinction between the life that is Christ-centered and the one that knows not God, only God Himself knows: but I have shown the paper to several of my non-Christian friends and it made more of an impact on them than anything I could say or do.

Our household shrank noticeably the last week of January. Harvey's parents who had provided a wonderful gift of time and moral support while with us returned to California. On the same day Tim, also, went back to Biola.

After Darryl's grandparents and brother left, we noticed that Darryl's unhealed incision had become infected. We, too, had to make a trip—back to the oncology clinic at Children's Hospital. He had a staph infection which required an antibiotic. This, in turn, precluded him from taking scheduled chemotherapy treatment on the following Friday.

On Thursday of that week, the principal of Dunstan Junior High along with two teachers and four students came to visit Darryl. They brought money that students and teachers had collected for him. Darryl beamed as one of the group handed him a check. He had heard news of a gift collected for him and had already concluded that through that gift God would provide the money for his Faith Promise.

Now, as he looked at the check in his hand, the amount overwhelmed him—$424.00! He bubbled over as he thanked them. "God used you to answer my prayer!" he said. Exuberantly, he told them that he now had the money, $250.00, for which he had prayed for that whole year. With that money he could fulfill the Faith Promise for missionary work that he had made at his church.

Beyond his excitement about the gift of money he received, Darryl delighted in seeing friends from his school, teachers, and his school principal. Excited conversation ensued as these friends tried to catch Darryl up on events at school.

Darryl delightedly gave the money fulfilling his Faith Promise on the following Sunday. This, in turn, opened up an opportunity for him to challenge others to trust God to provide for a Faith Promise. On Easter Sunday, the pastor asked him to share with the entire congregation of our church about the Faith Promise he had made the previous year. He shared how, in dependence on God, he had made a commitment beyond what he felt he could earn in the coming year. He had then prayed earnestly that God would provide what he had promised to give. He continued to pray—on his hospital bed—even after it was apparent that he was incapable of earning the money on his own. Then God had miraculously provided more than the full amount through the generosity of his fellow students at school. Darryl reemphasized how he had kept praying and believing that God would provide for him when it seemed totally impossible.

When he finished telling about the visit of his school friends and his response to the gift they had placed in his hand, the whole congregation broke out in spontaneous applause. People reflected genuine excitement by Darryl's testimony concerning God's faithfulness. Many also thought of the added miracle that Darryl still lived—able to give this testimony. At that time, Darryl looked so good physically it seemed unbelievable that he daily walked under a continuing threat of death. After the service, I asked Darryl if he had felt afraid to talk to that large crowd of over 800 people. He replied, "Well, no. I just felt kind of funny saying anything about my illness because I feel so well now."

On Saturday, Charlotte and Ray followed Tim back to school. We again expressed gratefulness for the generosity of Biola students who provided all of us a special lift by making their visit possible. Strangely, they had come home to tell Darryl "good-bye," but God opened a different door for him.

With increasing strength, Darryl faced the prospect of returning to school. Anxieties arising out of weeks of illness and isolation from his school friends tempered his desire to return. However, he planned to begin the following Monday if he continued to feel well enough and did not develop other complications.

In the midst of these changing circumstances, Darryl received an ongoing flow of letters. One letter came from Floyd M. Sack, a member of the Colorado House of Representatives. He wrote:

> I read of your illness in the Rocky Mountain News, and from the article also learned that you are a young man of great faith. Though God has given you an extra heavy burden to carry, you have faced up to it in the most courageous way.
>
> I am proud, Darryl, to think that I have known you in this small way for you have made many of us stop and think today is the day we should live and love the will of God.
>
> I send my blessings and prayers, and I know that God will be very close to you in the days ahead.

An older lady who lived in Lakewood called me on the phone. She had suffered as a semi-invalid for forty years, experiencing diabetes along with a bone disease, which caused her bones to break very easily. Having read Darryl's story in the paper, she called to tell me that it had given her special courage to face her own debilitating illness. Following up on that call she became acquainted with Darryl over the phone and called him often. As they got to know each other, she asked him to call her "Aunt Helen." She visited our home several times, and in turn, we visited her. A warm friendship developed between our families. She and Darryl carried on a periodic exchange of notes and phone calls. One poem that she sent Darryl on a card called Sweet Notes, reflected their relationship:

> The reason why we're such good friends
> Is very plain to see,
> I understand the things you do.
> You have respect for me;
> No complicated folk are we,
> No striving to be clever,
> Yes, friends may come and friends may go,
> But we'll be friends forever!

Their love and care for each other developed and Aunt Helen seemed to become an indivisible part of our family.

Another letter that Darryl received from someone in Denver encouraged him:

> You might be interested in knowing that I sent part of your last letter [he had had correspondence with this woman before because of the news article] to a cousin in Oregon who they had just discovered had cancer. He died just two weeks ago, but the last we heard, he had opened up and allowed two of my Christian aunts to talk to him and he had accepted Christ. Until he read your letter, he wouldn't allow anybody to even mention God to him. Thank you so much for all of your wonderful testimony.
>
> We think of you so often, Darryl. It's odd how you can feel so close to somebody you've never met. Sometimes during the night I've awakened and felt the need to pray for you. I know that

many lives have been changed because of you and the way you have trusted God.

In a unique way, that *Rocky Mountain News* article projected Darryl's story around the world. A woman sent a copy of the article to her friend, Nancy Woolnough, a staff person at radio station HCJB in Quito, Ecuador. From its location high in the Andes, HCJB's short wave signal projected into Africa, the Far East and all over South and North America.

Nancy attended The Bible Institute of Los Angeles (now Biola University) at the same time as Harvey and me. Although we had not maintained contact with her, she remembered us. The article had particularly intrigued her because she had produced a weekly program for over twelve years designed to help people as they or their loved ones faced death or dying.

She immediately wrote and requested that Harvey record an interview with Darryl that she could incorporate into her series. She went on to tell us that the series had already included "testimonies . . . of different folk, including the wives of the five missionaries killed by Auca Indians, articles from Time Magazine, nurses, doctors, Christian writers like Joseph Bailey and C. S. Lewis, National Observer etc." God again used the events in Darryl's life in ways that we could not have imagined.

Chapter 11

BACK TO SCHOOL

Encouraged by his doctors, Darryl returned to school. Six weeks had passed since he sat at any of his school desks. He went back on a parent-teacher conference day so he only had a half-day of school; but he discovered that even a half-day was quite traumatic. Interacting with so many people wore him out. Much had been made of his illness during his absence, and everyone had questions.

One boy wanted to know how many cigarettes Darryl had smoked. This young acquaintance had internalized the danger of smoking, but somehow missed the fact that many kinds of cancer exist with many different causes. Since Darryl had cancer, the boy assumed that he must have gotten it by smoking. Darryl told us that his schoolmate looked shocked when he told him that he had never even tried to smoke.

The darker side of human nature also reared its ugly head. A fellow student who had earlier shown disdain for Darryl's life and testimony met him in the hall. Other students watched as he intentionally put his foot out and tripped Darryl sending him sprawling across the hall. When kids glared at the boy for his insensitive action he yelled, "I didn't mean to. That was just an accident!"

The fall shook Darryl up. One of his friends told us later that he sat for a while on the floor before finding strength to get up and walk. He still felt weak from all he had been through and this tumble strained him physically.

However, Darryl, in his characteristic way, finally got up and went on his way merely expressing sorrow that the other student seemed to have a negative attitude toward him.

Other events during that half-day of school weighed on Darryl as well. A girl in his orchestra class told him that their teacher had talked to the class about him one day. I guess since the teacher expected that Darryl would never return to school, he expressed to the class the misfortune of a life of one as brilliant as Darryl being cut short. He said that Darryl's IQ may have surpassed any of the teachers at Dunstan. This information shocked Darryl. He had never thought much about his IQ, but hearing what she said had a profound effect on him. He told me about that surprising conversation later in the day. Instead of evidencing pride, Darryl said, "You know, Mother, if God has given me this much ability, it is really wrong for me to ever get a B in a class. I'm just not living up to my potential."

The intensity in our home increased at this pressure-filled time when the father of one of the students who boarded with us came to visit. We made space available for him, adding one more person to our already busy household. Soon we learned that our new guest had a strong commitment to faith healing. He took it upon himself to deride Darryl for his illness. He advised him that if he had more faith he would be healed. He pressed his point until it became very trying for Darryl. This continuing pressure hit him and the rest of the family particularly hard at the end of his difficult first day back at school.

Darryl's ongoing reintegration into school life coupled with unavoidable tensions in our home exacted an emotional toll on him. We had marveled at his ability to handle stress, but increasing pressures made him become tense and unsure of himself. As his uneasiness increased, he experienced fear of being alone in an irrational way. We recognized his uncharacteristic response but were not unduly surprised. His world had turned upside down. His illness had left him physically weak and emotionally spent—increased, no doubt, by some exotic medications so experimental that his doctors lacked knowledge concerning potential side effects.

These disappointing reactions led Darryl to blame himself and feel like he had failed to trust the Lord. I observed this happening and realized he needed help. Pressed hard enough, everyone comes to a breaking point—a place where emotional responses go beyond control. Adding medications that affect the emotions to the equation makes that much more likely.

Since I had experienced similar reactions a few years earlier, I felt that sharing my struggles might help Darryl understand the problems he confronted. "Darryl, you have to realize that it is not abnormal for you feel the way you do," I told him one day. "Your body is weak, you've lost lots of weight, and the medications have set your nerves on edge. I can sort of understand because I had a lot of the same feelings when I lost our little baby in Africa. I was so weak and so ill and, yes, I guess I nearly died. In my depressed state, I couldn't stand it any time Dad had to be away. In fact, whenever he left me, I convinced myself that I couldn't make it until he would return. When I met new people I found it very difficult. I even found it hard to be with friends that I'd known for a long time. I broke down and cried for no reason at all."

Darryl looked at me intently for a few minutes before bursting out, "Oh Mother, did that happen to you too? I'm so glad that you told me. Now I won't feel so guilty for having the kind of feelings that I've been having."

Adjusting back to school life took more time and effort than we had anticipated. In spite of the message I had communicated to Darryl, he continued to struggle with a sense of inadequacy. He could not control those nagging feelings. Compounding his emotional struggle, he started to have other physical problems as well. Medications caused constipation which then often caused a painful stomachache. Watching him in pain made it difficult for both Harvey and me. We wanted to help but didn't know how.

At that point, Darryl developed a new interest. He decided to buy an aquarium and some tropical fish with money left over from the gift given by his school friends. This also provided a helpful distraction for Harvey. He carried a full teaching and counseling load and had increasing opportunities for outside speaking. This helped pay the bills but he recognized that he needed to do something to break the emerging debilitating tension. It seemed wise to accomplish that goal by coupling it with Darryl's developing new interest.

Harvey and Darryl headed out the door to purchase needed equipment for this budding project when the phone rang. The man I had talked to on the day Darryl's story came out in the paper immediately began scolding Harvey for being such a cruel father—a father who would let his child suffer without reason. He again insisted that through his power of meditation he could heal Darryl. We sensed demonic opposition evident in such calls and recognized the negative effect they produced in us. Convinced that we did not need that kind of "help," Harvey gently extricated himself from this unwanted distraction and left with Darryl for their shopping trip.

While the girls played outside, I decided I had better get some of my ironing done. I had fallen so far behind. As I began, I pondered our situation. True, plenty of things could have made us feel depressed, but I also considered the special evidences of God's love that we had experienced in recent days. Why do we find it so difficult to rest in the knowledge of God's unfailing love? My mind returned to Harvey's phone call and the demonic pall it had cast over us. I realized that this provided a clue concerning the source of our struggles. God had worked—and continued to work—through the incredible newspaper article concerning Darryl. Many people continued to come to Christ through that article. Why wouldn't Satan, then, seek to oppress and defeat us by every means at his disposal? We needed to expect that a Satanic attack could follow.

As I continued to iron and think, the commands of James 4:6-10 came to mind. "Draw near to God," and "resist the Devil." The Bible tells us that when we resist the Devil, he flees from us. At the same time, as we draw near to God, He draws near to us. As I began to praise God for his promised provision and care in time of need, the load lifted. I spent the next hour in prayer as I transformed that stack of wrinkled clothing into hangers full of freshly ironed garments.

Feeling an inexplicable release, I continued to pour out my heart in praise to God. This led to me praying for many others with known difficulties for whom God had burdened me. As I continued to spend time in God's presence, He brought one of my favorite scriptures to mind. Second Corinthians 2:14 proclaims, "Now thanks be unto God, which always causeth us to triumph in Christ and maketh manifest the savor of his knowledge by us in every place." Since God "always causes us to triumph . . . in every place," I could even thank Him for the eerie phone call that had set this reverie of thought in motion which God used to open my eyes anew to Him and to His works. Why had I forgotten that I battled not against flesh and blood but against principalities and powers—indeed, the very Evil One, himself? Thank God, "greater is He that is in [me], than He that is in the world" (I John 4:4)

As I sat alone with Harvey later that evening, I told him about the great time I had spent with the Lord while he and Darryl went shopping. Harvey, too, felt the heaviness of spiritual warfare. Convinced that Satan himself delivered special attacks on us in these days, I related some of the truths that God had used to speak to my heart. Consequently, in spite of the many demands on our time that seemed to consume us, we recognized the need to make more time to obey and draw near to God as James 4 commands us. Harvey got up earlier than normal the following morning and went down to his study in the basement. He spent a long time alone with our Heavenly Father. Returning upstairs for breakfast after that time in prayer, he told me, "Honey, the burden has lifted."

When Darryl went to the oncology clinic for his next scheduled checkup, we received good news. Darryl always had to stop first at the lab to have blood drawn for tests scheduled that week. The blood tests showed marked improvement. Even Lori Chesler, the pleasant young lady who handled the paperwork at the lab window, expressed enthusiasm by the encouraging report. Lori seemed challenged by Darryl's life. During the months of his treatment, a special friendship between her and our whole family developed.

Darryl also had chest x-rays that day which further encouraged us. The x-rays showed *no* sign of fluid in his lungs. In fact, his doctors told us that because of the progress shown, they decided to discontinue use of two of his medications. Furthermore, they said that the following week he could begin to come in *every other* week instead of *every* week for chemotherapy. They indicated that he had completed the worst part of his treatment, and that he should continue to feel better day by day. His primary medication, prednisone, had caused Darryl to develop a moon face; they assured him that he would now begin to look more normal. This extended to his hair which, although it had not completely fallen out, it had thinned.

While I went to the hospital pharmacy to pick up Darryl's medicine during this clinic visit, the staff questioned him about a number of things. To questions such as, "Does it bother you that you have this disease? And do you worry about it?" Darryl quickly responded, "No it doesn't bother me and I don't worry about it because God has permitted it. I am willing for whatever God has for me in allowing this disease."

"But how about your parents, don't they worry about it?" they asked.

"No, they feel the same way that I do about it."

"Well, if you ever feel like telling us something that you don't feel you can tell your parents, feel free to talk to us about it." Thankfully, Darryl *did* feel free to talk to me and told me what they had said as we traveled home.

He then went on, "You know people like them just can't understand the freedom we kids have to talk to you about anything, because our family is different. It's even different than most of the other church families because we can really talk to each other." I felt so grateful that God had enabled me to build that kind of a relationship with our kids long before this time of stress had come upon us.

Darryl's comments encouraged me. I tried to allow our children the freedom to speak about whatever might be on their hearts. I still treasured the uncanny skill my dad had shown in maintaining a climate that made me feel comfortable in talking with him; I wanted that same kind of open relationship with each of our children.

I wanted to model something else for our children but realized that I often fell short. Thinking back to lessons with which I had struggled when baby Donny died, God spoke to me again through I Thessalonians 5:18, "In everything give thanks: for this is the will of God in Christ Jesus concerning you." Although difficult because of the trauma of Darryl's illness, I prayed for and worked at maintaining a thankful spirit. I desired God's help that I might daily grow in my ability to thank Him, honestly, for the "everythings" in my life. This could be possible only through God's wonderful, daily provision of His grace. I deeply desired that my life, and responses to what God allowed in my life, might become a tool to teach each of our children to learn to trust God in the difficult times of their lives.

Our friends at the clinic could not understand my attitude, but God provided me with an increasing sense of His peace and joy. That joy often arose out of deep emotional and spiritual struggles. God's sustaining grace in these circumstances exceeded my natural understanding. In a way that I had never experienced before, I yearned to see my Savior, Jesus Christ, face to face. Maybe that is what prompted a friend to remark one day, "For some reason, Evadene, your face just seems to shine."

Darryl gradually increased his activities. He enjoyed returning to church after missing services for two months. Getting back to this regular part of Darryl's life and participating in his Sunday School class again excited him.

In all of his suffering and struggle, Darryl had not lost his zest for living or his fun-loving spirit. Children's Hospital catered to small children, their largest group of patients, by filling the place with juvenile pictures and play things. As a teenager, Darryl noted and mentioned to me that one of his doctors had worn an ABC and number tie. In talking to Dr. Wuri, I mentioned that Darryl had expressed amusement at his tie and its juvenile nature. A good-natured fellow, he responded, "Okay then, I won't wear it on the days that Darryl comes in." He didn't forget, but also teased Darryl because he didn't like his tie.

A few days later, Harvey took Darryl to the clinic. On the way home they stopped at Villa Italia Shopping Center in Lakewood. In a shop window they saw a pair of men's shorts covered with hearts. Harvey teased, "There, Darryl! You should get a pair of shorts like that to wear when you're getting examined at the clinic. That would stop them."

Without missing a beat, Darryl responded, "No way, Dad. I want a pair of shorts with ABC's on them."

"Hey," Harvey shot back, "maybe you've got something there!" They shared their wild conversation with me when they returned home and the project began. I headed out to the shopping center and bought some ABC material and a pattern. By Darryl's next visit to the clinic, he wore some striking undershorts.

Harvey and I both accompanied him to the clinic on that visit. The doctors had told us that they needed blood samples from each of us as well as from Darryl's younger sisters for some added research. They also checked our blood for the existence of certain antibodies.

I waited in the room with Darryl when they began to examine him. As usual, he had changed into a hospital gown for his examination. When the doctor pulled up the hospital gown, he howled. He didn't even try to go on with the examination but ran out of the room to find Dr. Wuri, the doctor who had started all of this by wearing his ABC tie. Locating Dr. Wuri, he insisted that he needed to examine Darryl that day. Not understanding why, Dr. Wuri made his way into the examining room. With obvious concern he observed Darryl intently as he pulled up his hospital gown. When he saw the shorts he came unglued. With a hysterical whoop, he ran out of the room to find Dr. Holton, the doctor in charge of the clinic. She walked into the room, also wondering what kind of problem had arisen. She pulled up Darryl's hospital gown and the boisterous laughter began all over again. Word of Darryl's daring apparel spread like wildfire throughout the ward and provided a light moment that eased the normal somber environment.

Our fun didn't stop there. With Valentine's Day approaching, I found a Valentine card for Darryl that, with some tinkering, suited the oncology staff. I cut out a little tie and under shorts from the same ABC material which I had used for Darryl's shorts and glued this on the person on the Valentine. With appropriate fanfare, he presented this card to the staff the following week. Needless to say, that brought down the house again. It helped everyone to enjoy a moment of fun in that usually tense hospital atmosphere.

Darryl loved to have fun but he put forth even greater effort in another aspect of his life. He exhibited an overriding goal to learn to know his Heavenly Father and to walk in obedience to Him. For over a year, Harvey and Darryl had an in-depth weekly Bible study. This daily study and the discussions with his dad that grew out of their weekly meeting helped Darryl in his Christian growth. Darryl earnestly sought to obey God's Word. As God spoke to him through His Word, we often saw noticeable changes in his life. He demonstrated his desire to become Christ-like in his daily walk. I perceived that this also helped him to face the problems of his illness that included the potential for an early and untimely death. Knowing the Lord Jesus as he did created within him a deep longing to see his Savior face to face.

Chapter 12

FAMILY CHALLENGES PERSIST

*I*n spite of my desire to meet the spiritual and emotional needs of *each* of the children in our family, I realized how easily I missed attaining that goal. At some point during those hectic days, my mother observed in one of her good letters that I rarely mentioned Faith or Susan in my letters. She asked me, "Why?" That question made me realize that I had not only failed to write about them, I had also failed to spend enough time with them. Darryl's illness and meeting his needs consumed my life. Her observation called this to my attention and I attempted to spend more quality time with them. They needed me too!

Susan counted down the days until her sixth birthday—a big day on her calendar. Birthday children in her kindergarten class received special attention on *their* day including a birthday crown to wear throughout the morning. Often short-changed at home as we cared for Darryl, she needed this extra attention. Did all of that, perhaps, lay the groundwork for what happened next?

When she arrived home from school that afternoon, she ushered her father into our bedroom for a special consultation. Looking up into his face, she informed him, "Now that I am six, I won't need the hall light on anymore when I go to bed. The little night light in my room will be enough. And Daddy, I'm going to eat my food right away, so I don't lose my dessert."

She included other things also that she promised to do to improve her behavior. Serious about her words, she took immediate action evidenced in a dramatic change in her eating habits. Needless to say, this affected discipline matters, something that both Susan and her dad appreciated.

Having Darryl feeling better gave more time to concentrate on meeting the girls' physical and spiritual needs. They appreciated Darryl's return to his basement bedroom. They had accepted the need to move in together to allow Darryl to have an upstairs bedroom during his time of need, but that didn't mean that they liked sleeping in the same bed. They had experienced the luxury of each having a bedroom, so living together had produced friction more than once. Therefore, everyone had a sense of relief when Darryl moved back to his own room.

Nevertheless, this did not halt sibling rivalry. One night I let Faith and Susan watch *Winnie the Pooh* on our small TV. When the story ended Susan jumped up and turned off the TV. Faith immediately reacted by turning it back on; she wanted to see the end of the Sear's advertisement. Susan, determined to have it her way, scratched Faith's face and eyes. I reprimanded Susan for her aggressive behavior and told her that she would have to dry all the dishes by herself instead of sharing the job with Faith as usual. Susan cried most of the time she dried dishes. At the same time, Faith laid on the living room floor crying because of her wounds—or hurt feelings. With my energy already spent, listening to all of this commotion as I washed dishes didn't help. After completing the dishes, I sent the girls to their rooms to put on their nighties.

They returned to the living room ready for bed. Following my usual practice, I read a chapter from their Bible story book before reading from another book that would help to teach some important lesson of life. That night I continued to read from Faith's book entitled *Bird Life in Wington*. The next chapter portrayed two birds that got their feathers ruffled because one displayed jealousy of the pretty feather worn in the other bird's hat. Her jealousy led to gossip about her neighbor. As a result both birds expressed anger with each other.

After the story I talked to the girls about their foolishness in fighting over such a little thing as the commercial on TV. They acted as ridiculous as the two birds in the story. I then suggested that Susan ask Faith for forgiveness for scratching her, and I asked Faith to grant Susan forgiveness. They did not hesitate and both did as I suggested. But Susan still wanted to have the last word so added, "I just made a mistake."

"No," I responded, "You didn't just make a mistake." Susan looked at me with surprise, so I asked her, "Do you know what you did?"

"What?"

"That was sin, and because of sin such as this, Christ had to die on the cross."

As I prayed with her after she crawled into her bed, I told her that I appreciated that she had asked Faith for forgiveness but she needed to ask God to forgive her also. To hear her name the sin she had committed and ask God to forgive her for it provided me assurance of progress in learning a needed lesson. I had asked God to show me some growth and evidence of spiritual understanding in Faith and Susan. To see God working in their young lives brought me great joy.

Out of his disciplined life, Darryl also grew concerned as he noticed areas of perceived lack in his younger sisters. He desired to see them get more involved in reading the Bible for themselves. As their older brother, he felt responsible for their spiritual growth and development. He shared his concern with me one day and asked for advice on what he could do to help Faith and Susan see that they needed to know God in a more intimate way.

Thankful for his evident concern but also recognizing some implicit danger, I told him, "Darryl, the very best thing you can do to help your sisters to love God is to show your love for them." Recognizing that when Darryl saw a perceived problem he sometimes attempted to straighten his sisters out, I continued, "Probably, Darryl, trying to correct your younger sisters will tend to make them angry rather than pointing them to Christ. If you avoid 'bossing' them and try to consistently show love, you will get much further in helping them to know and love God."

Darryl heeded my advice and made a conscious effort to show and express his love for both of his sisters. This proved to be a great help in both of their lives—and in our home.

Stimulated by Darryl's concern for his sisters' discipline, I reflected back several years when God had dealt with me about disciplining our children. Thankfully, I had obeyed God's leading. I considered the added difficulty Darryl would have experienced if he had embarked on this road of illness and vulnerability without the discipline he had built into his life. Now he yearned to see his sisters build discipline into their lives. I would not have a story to write if Darryl hadn't learned those lessons early in life.

Along with Darryl's disciplined life, we noted a deepening thoughtfulness in his consideration for others. He got up early in the morning while Faith still slept in the next room and exhibited caring concern for her by using his tape recorder in the memorization of scripture. To check the accuracy of his memorization he recorded the memorized passage, but in a whisper, so as not to disturb Faith as she continued sleeping.

Darryl often increased pressure on himself in his approach to school assignments. He toiled over a massive report for his language arts class. While they studied the Civil War, the teacher assigned each student an oral report on some aspect of the war. Darryl chose to do his research and report on Abraham Lincoln. Looking to do something a little out of the ordinary, he recorded his whole report on a tape recorder, including musical background and appropriate sound effects. He "borrowed" his father's voice to speak the words of Abraham Lincoln. He coordinated the taped report with illustrations and pictures that he had drawn or copied to be shown on a screen. By carefully arranging his materials, he produced an outstanding and interesting report. He received many compliments for this project from his classmates and his teacher. With this big project behind him, he concentrated on making up remaining school work from the many weeks he had missed.

Living in an area subject to unexpected major changes in weather presented other kinds of challenges. Because the weather man predicted a huge snow storm one day, Harvey decided that he should take my place in making the six-mile trip to Children's Hospital in Denver for Darryl's required treatment. He left at 1:30 PM, expecting to be back by 4:30 or 5:00 at the latest. In the lab that day, they drew an extra large vial of blood to send to the research center in Washington DC. They also planned to send a specimen of Darryl's bone marrow. The doctor scheduled to perform the bone marrow sample had to leave on an emergency call to Glenwood Springs which delayed the procedure.

As the medical team continued Darryl's examination, they expressed concern because his reflexes seemed sluggish. They asked him to do several unusual things such as walking on his toes like a ballet dancer. Checking his reflexes further with their little mallet below his knee, they concluded that his medicine, vincristine, had slowed his reflexes. Harvey found this conclusion more encouraging than their original suspicion that cancer had penetrated his nervous system.

The business office delayed Harvey longer than expected with questions concerning some insurance problems. Dr. Holton kept Darryl busy during this time, prodding him to share his feelings. She seemed concerned, in particular, about how returning to school had affected him. Since they had discontinued his prednisone, we presumed that she sought to determine the difference this made in his ability to cope with stress.

By the time Dr. Holton completed her interaction with Darryl, the early analysis of his bone marrow had come back from the lab. With this good lab report, his doctors decided to delay Darryl's next chemotherapy treatment for a week. Harvey wanted to talk to Dr. Holton but the various complicating factors of the afternoon had already delayed them more than seemed wise in light of the approaching storm. In fact, the latest weather reports coming over the radio in the waiting room indicated that heavy snow had closed many area roads as the storm increased in intensity. Harvey decided that he needed to wait for another visit to talk with Dr. Holton. Waiting any longer may have prevented them from being able to leave at all. He feared that the fallen snow might already make their six-mile trip to Lakewood difficult.

Then, to Harvey's dismay, he found a dead car battery because he had forgotten to turn off his headlights. Thankfully, God provided a good Samaritan who saw his need and gave him a jump. This enabled them to get on their way without too much delay.

However, after exiting the parking lot, Harvey discovered icy streets were taking their toll. Several smashed, disabled vehicles blocked the street. Caught in the resultant traffic jam which impeded progress, the idling motor died. They had traveled only two blocks from the hospital. No matter what he tried, the car would not start. Harvey knew that he dare not keep Darryl out in this frigid cold in his weakened condition, so he took him into a restaurant to keep him warm. It was already 6:30 PM. Harvey called to tell me what had happened and let me know that they would not arrive home for some time. He planned to leave Darryl in the restaurant while he tried to find someone to help get the car started.

With supper already getting cold when Harvey called, I decided not to wait any longer. After Susan, Faith and I ate, I told Faith to wash the dishes and gave Susan the privilege of drying them. With snow accumulated over 18 inches on our steep sloping driveway, I knew that I had to do something to enable Harvey to get into the garage when he finally arrived home.

I had spent considerable time clearing that pile of snow when to my relief, Butch, our neighbor boy who had taken over Darryl's paper route, saw my plight and came out to help me finish the job. I appreciated his help—and his company—so very much. I had been clearing snow for over an hour. Butch and I had nearly finished when I saw the lights of the car laboriously approaching down the street. Our home in the Green Mountain area sat on the ascending foothills of the Rocky Mountains so Harvey planned his approach carefully. Snowplows had not yet cleared the uphill streets in proximity to our home, so he had taken a cleared street to a point higher than our home. This enabled him, with the help of studded tires, to descend to our driveway. It worked. An overwhelming sense of relief washed over me as, at last, I saw our car creeping down through the still-blowing snow. With the driveway cleared, Harvey could drive straight into our garage. In all, the usual 30-minute drive home took them 3 1/2 hours. At this late hour, hunger gripped them. Yet we all felt thankful that they had made it home safely. As I reflected on the day, I gratefully acknowledged Harvey's wisdom in deciding to take Darryl to the doctor. I don't know if I could have made it home.

In a remarkable way Darryl exhibited unusual responsiveness and submission to God through the hurdles of his ongoing cancer, but he also struggled with frustrations arising out of his lengthy illness. At one point he wrote a letter to his sister, Charlotte, expressing dissatisfaction because he could not get caught up. He said:

> Right now, I'm really praying that you are praying for me. I guess I'm kind of going through a stage that comes many times after being in the hospital for some time, then trying to get back into things. It seems that in homework and letter writing, I'm just spinning my wheels hopelessly. Please pray that I will be spinning my wheels with my hope centered on our Lord Jesus Christ.
>
> Char, so many times I wonder why I'm not in heaven right now singing praises to my Lord. Then comes the answer. God wanted me to praise Him on earth at the present time for reasons that I, as a human should not question, nor could not understand. Do I really measure up to what God wanted me to be on this earth? God is doing so much. I'll have to write about that in the letter I write to the boys. Share this with my other big siblings.

Challenges to our family came from many directions during those intense days. While Darryl appeared well, we felt uncertain about what his

113

doctors thought. We sensed that they anticipated that regressive symptoms could reoccur at any time. A call from the oncology clinic advising me that they now offered a program in psychological hypnosis therapy reinforced my feelings. My caller insisted that Darryl participate in this biweekly program. She explained that children could reduce their anxieties and concerns by learning to respond to hypnosis.

We tried to maintain open communication with Darryl's doctors. We assumed that they recommended this training because he had experienced tension, including severe headaches, as he adjusted back to school life. We wanted to help Darryl in any way we could but felt uneasy about this new program. To emphasize the power of hypnosis, she explained that its usage successfully helped hemophiliacs to control bleeding. She also commented on the anticipated usefulness of hypnosis to control pain in the later stages of cancer treatment. Somewhat shaken by the implication of what might lie ahead I responded that I needed to talk to my husband about these things.

When Harvey got home that afternoon I told him about my phone conversation. As we talked, he also voiced indefinable reservations similar to those that gripped me. Unable to identify why we felt as we did, we both agreed that we should not allow Darryl to participate in the program unless we learned additional things about it that might change our minds. We would continue to pray for God's direction concerning our decision.

I called the clinic the next day and told them that we decided we did not want Darryl to participate in the program. Almost unbelieving, the nurse wanted to know why we didn't want this help. I told her that Darryl had coped with his problems quite well. When things bothered him, we talked them out with him which decreased his anxieties. I also told her that we would like to speak with Dr. Holton to gain a better understanding of what benefits Darryl might receive by participating in the program; we felt open to reevaluating our decision as we received further information.

When I took Darryl to the clinic for his next scheduled appointment, Mrs. Clapp, the nurse who had called me, indicated that Dr. Holton's full schedule made her unavailable for a conference. She then pressed me about my hesitations. I felt this opened the door for me to ask some questions with which I struggled. "When do you consider a person in remission? Do you consider Darryl presently in remission?"

"When the tumor mass decreased in Darryl's groin we considered him in remission."

"Then how can we tell if Darryl continues in remission? What should we look for that might indicate change?"

"If the tumors come back or if the disease spills over into a full blown leukemia, which it most often does, he will be out of remission."

"Do you consider that Darryl presently has leukemia then?"

Rather slowly, she said, "No, he now has lymphosarcoma. *Sarcoma* refers to the tumor masses, and *lympho* means that it is in the lymph system."

It helped me to receive answers to these questions that I had mulled over in my mind. But then, I returned to the starting point of our discussion, "Since you consider Darryl in remission at present, why do you want him to join these sessions on hypnosis?"

"We believe that hypnosis provides many possible positive results. Through hypnosis, children may control the sick feeling some of them experience with their vincristine injections. You may have observed that some children start throwing up as soon as they get into the hospital parking lot, even before they come into the clinic."

"Darryl has never had this problem, so I don't see why he should need the hypnosis therapy."

Looking at me with obvious deep concern the nurse said, "Mrs. Stranske, I want you to know that if Darryl's cancer resurfaces, either in the same glands where it first appeared or deeper within his abdomen, it will cause *honest-to-God* pain. If it gets to that place, therapy will do no good. Frankly, that is what we fear, and that is why we believe that introducing Darryl to the techniques of hypnosis could provide a powerful tool to deal with such pain." Then, seeming to realize what she had said, and seeking to soften the blow of her strong words somewhat, she continued, "But maybe it will never come back. We simply can't predict."

I had not realized before, or perhaps had not thought about the developing potential, that this dread disease could progress to a place where it would cause such extreme pain. I thought that a return of Darryl's cancer might again cause his lungs to fill with fluid depriving him of needed oxygen and so, eventually, suffocate him. The heartbreaking and grim possibility of unmanageable pain just described by Mrs. Clapp hit me very hard, filling me with a foreboding kind of fear of all that might lie ahead. By contrast, we had noted that Darryl looked better in recent days after getting off his prednisone treatment. His puffy checks returned to normal and he gained weight. In fact, he weighed almost one hundred pounds again.

When I returned home from the clinic that day I shared the things I had learned with Harvey. In spite of the dire warning about possible debilitating pain, we both felt convinced that we should not involve Darryl in this hypnosis program. We recognized that our underlying concern related to those who would take control of Darryl's thought processes through such hypnosis. We appreciated every one of the doctors that worked with great diligence to effect healing in Darryl's body, but we didn't know if any of these caring, committed individuals knew our God in the way Darryl knew Him. We feared that a doctor who did not know God might, in his or her manipulation of Darryl's mind, turn Darryl away from his dependence upon God. For us, this danger outweighed any kind of possible physical pain.

The events of the last day or two left me feeling anxious and depressed. I grappled with the persistent desire of our doctors to utilize hypnosis as part of their treatment. Although convinced that we made the right decision, my concern that we do nothing to hinder needed treatment for Darryl persisted. I knew that I couldn't accomplish anything else until I had spent some time in the Word of God and prayer.

I opened my Bible to Psalm 41:1-3 through which God had spoken so clearly to me during Darryl's hospital stay. Meditating on those verses again,

I thought about my prayer and God's leading that night. I still believed that God would preserve Darryl and keep him alive. But then, torn by the thought that God may allow this cancer to spread before He healed him and Darryl would have extreme pain, I wondered again, "Might I deprive Darryl of something that he really needed?" It tears a mother's heart out to see her child in pain and feel helpless to do anything about it.

Once more, the promise of Psalms 41:3 quieted my spirit as I absorbed what God said to me right then when I so desperately needed it, "The Lord will strengthen him upon the bed of languishing; thou wilt make all his bed in his sickness." God, Himself, would strengthen Darryl and meet his needs even on his bed of sickness. Peace filled my heart and mind as the conviction overwhelmed me that we could trust our all-wise and loving Heavenly Father and believe Him for the results. We should not risk entrusting Darryl's God-sustained mind to the finite wisdom of doctors. With that, I turned to Philippians 4:7 and reveled anew in that precious promise: "And the peace of God which passeth all understanding shall keep your hearts and minds through Christ Jesus." I felt comforted in believing that God could and would give Darryl—and me—His abiding grace for any time of pain that might lie ahead. Beyond that, God would provide enduring peace and keep Darryl's heart and mind stayed on Him regardless of the circumstances he might face.

After I spent this time of communion with my Heavenly Father, I went to work in the kitchen and cleaned up the dishes. I kept singing the chorus our older children had taught us:

> I've got confidence,
> God is going to see me through,
> No matter what the case may be,
> I know He's going to fix it for me.[6]

---

[6] "I've Got Confidence" by Andrae' Crouch. Copyright © 1969 Bud John Songs (ASCAP) (adm. at EM!CMGPublishing.com) All rights reserved. Used by permission. International Copyright Secured. All Rights Reserved. Used by Permission.

With a renewed peace of mind, I wrote to Charlotte:

> I'm so glad that I have a grown daughter who loves the Lord, with whom I can share all these deep things of my heart. I have the same thanks for mature sons, Ray and Tim, who want God first in their lives. It makes this period of testing so much easier to bear, because I can write to you kids and know that you will understand and that you will pray for us. I do love you so very much.

Throughout all of this time of personal struggle, we desired to glorify God through our lives. We wanted our lives to show forth Christ to the doctors at the clinic. We wanted God to use us and the experiences that He allowed into our lives to touch those doctors so that those who did not know our God might open their hearts to Him.

The next time I took Darryl to the clinic I reaffirmed to our doctors that we had decided against having Darryl participate in the psychological hypnosis program. I could feel their displeasure with our decision and their belief that we had made a wrong choice. They believed that our decision would cost us, and especially Darryl, when he needed added help for pain. We, on the other hand, experienced God's peace in our decision. Again, we committed our way into God's hands, and asked Him to enable us to show by our lives and demeanor that His power and His grace met every need both for our lives and for Darryl's.

People often misunderstood Darryl's singleness of purpose as well. He continued to excel in school in spite of numerous absences. He also started to catch up on missed assignments making him feel more comfortable with school life. About this time, a teacher gave an assignment to choose an occupation that might interest him as his life work. Students were to research their chosen occupation and then write an extensive paper about it. The teacher instructed them to explain the kind of work involved in this vocation, along with the expected remuneration and preparation required.

Darryl chose the vocation of a Missionary Bible Translator. He did a great job of researching this occupation and spent many hours in writing an excellent paper about this out-of-the-ordinary vocation. Of course, the fact that his parents had done missionary translation work may have had something to do with the focus of his interest. However, he chose the topic, a vocation we discovered he had considered for some time. In spite of the hours of painstaking work Darryl put into this project, his teacher gave him a B on the project. Reflecting a worldview very different from Darryl's, his teacher explained that Darryl's chosen vocation lacked the potential for providing sufficient remuneration to make it worth considering.

This teacher's materialistic approach saddened us. He based his grade on Darryl's choice of goals in life rather than on the effort and excellent work put into completing the assignment. Undeterred by this lower grade, Darryl expressed confidence that he had completed his assignment faithfully.

Chapter 13

BECKONED BY A GRADUATION
WE VACATION IN CALIFORNIA

*I*n mid-April our thoughts turned towards Charlotte's June graduation from Biola College. We missed Ray's January graduation because Darryl's tests at that time revealed the serious character of his illness. As Charlotte's graduation approached we again questioned the advisability of going. Darryl's doctors encouraged us, assuring us that they could work out details for him to receive necessary treatment in California; but we didn't have sufficient money to make the trip. We began praying that God would provide necessary funds if His purpose for us included attending Charlotte's graduation.

If our proposed trip became a reality, we wanted to go beyond the Los Angeles area. Most of Harvey's immediate family lived in proximity to the Biola campus in La Mirada, but my family lived 300 miles north of Los Angeles in Turlock. To our surprise, even this did not create a problem for obtaining Darryl's required treatment. One of his doctors had a friend and former schoolmate practicing in Turlock. He assured us that this doctor knew the necessary procedures that would enable him to administer Darryl's chemotherapy, and Children's Hospital in Los Angeles could provide treatment there.

We faced another dilemma. The Jefferson County school year ended after Charlotte's scheduled graduation. Because Darryl had already missed so much school, Harvey considered it unwise to take him out of school early. This meant that we needed to find someone with whom Darryl could stay to complete the semester. Although joining us later caused Darryl to miss Charlotte's graduation, he could visit his grandparents in southern California and travel with us to visit my family.

Continuing to work on various aspects of our expanding puzzle, we discovered that Darryl could fly from Denver to Los Angles on a student stand-by ticket for only $25.00. We also checked with Harvey's parents and found that we could borrow their small travel trailer, enabling us to keep costs down while incorporating some restful vacation into our trip. Harvey had experienced a demanding year and he needed time to relax. The more we thought and prayed about these matters, the more we saw the profit of such a trip if God enabled us to go.

Then, Susan became ill, and I took her to see Dr. Kurtz. Since I had not seen him for some weeks, he greeted me with, "How is Darryl, Mrs. Stranske?" I informed him of Darryl's apparent progress; then told him about the pressure put on us by the clinic staff to submit Darryl to their psychological hypnosis therapy. I further shared how we had agonized over our decision. Wondering how he would respond, I told Dr. Kurtz that we decided not to admit Darryl into this program, realizing that this meant that we needed to accept the fact that Darryl might experience great pain at some later point if God allowed his disease to progress. I added that we felt it important to trust God to meet the needs of whatever pain Darryl might suffer rather than entrust his thought processes into the hands of men or women who may not know our God. This kind, Christian doctor looked at me for some time before replying that he believed we made the right decision.

Encouraged by his response, I went on to say, "You know, Dr. Kurtz, maybe God will take Darryl through this whole illness and then heal him."

After a long pause and with tears in his eyes he said, "Mrs. Stranske, you need to recognize this as a period of temporary relief. I don't know if they have told you this at the clinic, but I received an update several days ago. Their bulletin indicated that they have diagnosed four cases of lymphosarcoma this year; only three of those patients are still living."

By this, Dr. Kurtz tried to tell me not to expect medical recovery. He did not want me to get my hopes up only to have them dashed. His words cut through me like a knife. I appreciated Dr. Kurtz's honesty along with the fact that, even in his forthright approach, he showed so much compassionate concern for me as a person. Thankfully, Susan only had another case of treatable strep throat, but the exchange with Dr. Kurtz continued to haunt me. When I got home, I felt washed out, almost devoid of the potential to function like a person. I fell on my knees before God, asking Him to give me His peace. And He did.

About this time, perhaps as a result of my interaction with Dr. Kurtz, I wrote my mother. My letter revealed my ongoing struggles:

> Just because Darryl is doing so well now, we still have no promise, medically speaking, that he is going to make it. This illness can pop out in different places at any time. But we have more than medicine; we have a God who is the God of the impossible, and we are trusting that He will rid Darryl's body of this cancer.

It didn't surprise me that, with all the pressure Harvey had encountered, he came down with the flu. He took one day off and then forced himself to teach his classes the following day. A few days later he awoke in the middle of the night, groaning, clutching his right side in terrible pain. Now what? I tried to call Dr. Kurtz, but got his partner, Dr. Hoffer. After I explained Harvey's intense pain to the best of my ability, Dr. Hoffer told me to take Harvey to the hospital emergency room.

Before we left for the hospital I awoke Darryl and asked him to come upstairs and sleep in our bed. Sometimes one of the girls would get frightened during the night and come into our bedroom for comfort. Thankfully, I took this precaution, because Susan did awaken and find Darryl in our bedroom. He told her what had happened, comforted her—and she went back to sleep.

When we arrived at Emergency, Dr. Hoffer took time to examine Harvey. After considering various possible options, he felt quite certain that Harvey had a kidney stone. He gave Harvey an injection to control pain and then took an x-ray. When the x-ray did not provide conclusive evidence confirming his diagnosis, he considered admitting Harvey to the hospital. However, the pain medication began to work, so he gave Harvey some Demerol pills for possible reoccurring pain and sent him home. Our emergency room trip had taken over three hours and we longed for sleep. Because daylight saving's time began that night I had expected a short night—but not that short.

On Monday, Harvey continued to feel weak and had a headache but insisted that he could teach the one class he had that day. By holding onto the podium to steady himself, he made it through the hour before returning to see the doctor. Concerned with the lack of a definitive diagnosis, the doctor admitted Harvey to the hospital for further tests. He wanted to be sure that the pain had not stemmed from a developing tumor on Harvey's kidney. More x-rays and other tests revealed nothing, causing Dr. Hoffer to conclude that a kidney stone had, in fact, produced Harvey's pain. He explained that the stone must have passed prior to the x-ray. He added that, once this process has started, kidneys often continue to produce other stones. Therefore, he would need to watch for symptoms that indicated a repetition of the process. Time proved the accuracy of his diagnosis.

These additional ongoing issues did not strengthen the case for going to California, and we continued to lack funds for the trip. But our hearts drew us to take part in this special celebration. Time was running out. We knew we needed to make our decision soon. Our choices would also impact the plans of our three California students. Struggling with all of this, I again set aside time to pray for God to show us what we should do.

On that very day, soon after I had spent time in praying for God's wisdom, my brother Wilbur called and said that they had sold my mother's house. From the money received, they planned to send us $100.00. He added that they were also sending a $25.00 gift for our 25th wedding anniversary.

When I checked our mail, I found a letter from Charlotte containing a $20.00 bill that someone had given her to send to us. Adding these gifts together, Harvey and I realized that they would enable us to purchase the two new tires we needed with enough left over to pay for Darryl's stand-by plane ticket. Overjoyed, we believed that God's provision of these gifts provided confirmation that we should plan to go. We needed additional funds, but we now felt confident that God would supply what we lacked.

Ecstatic, Darryl looked forward to making that plane trip all on his own. Prior to the receipt of those gifts some friends of ours invited him to stay with them for his final days of school. They also offered to take him to the airport. God continued to graciously meet our needs.

I maintained a grueling schedule in the days before our departure. Faith and Susan needed clothes for warmer weather, so I sewed them several shorts and tops. I also had to think through the clothes that Darryl required. In addition to thinking of things suitable for California, he needed school clothes for Colorado.

Harvey, too, planned ahead. He produced a weekly radio program, *Missionary News of the World*, for KWBI, our Western Bible Institute radio station. He had completed several of these fifteen-minute programs but needed to produce four more before we left. In between other duties, he prepared our car for the long trip ahead.

Finally, departure day arrived. We dropped Darryl off at our friends' house and left authorization for them to make necessary decisions about him in case of an emergency. We hoped they would not need to use it.

Soon after departing for California it felt like we had forgotten something. Without Darryl, we all felt just a little empty. We missed his pleasing banter.

I couldn't help but think, "Is this the way it would feel if Darryl didn't make it through his illness?"

We had an ice chest full of food to eat on the way. I had prepared sandwiches so we could eat in the car while we drove. As children aged ten and six are prone to do, Faith and Susan soon tired of each other's company in the close quarters of our car. When I scolded them for their impatience with each other, Susan responded, "The trouble is, Mom, Darryl's not here and he's the one that always helps us settle our fights."

Ouch. Darryl's absence resurfaced. As I thought about what Susan had said, I had to agree. Darryl often served as peacemaker in their childhood disputes.

Graduation-related festivities began with an alumni banquet scheduled the evening after we arrived. Since both Harvey and I graduated from Biola, we had a great time interacting with old friends from our past. We also tried to briefly catch up with our three college age children interrupting them from their busy end-of-year schedules.

We enjoyed the privilege of observing Charlotte's graduation the following afternoon. After the ceremony, we went to a reception at the home of Mrs. MacIntosh (affectionately called, Mrs. Mac, by Biola students). She had served with AIM in Congo while we worked in the Sudan. Charlotte and many other MKs (missionary kids) considered her home a wonderful haven.

A few days later we picked Darryl up at the Los Angeles airport. With Darryl's arrival, we tested our RVing skills by taking a short trip to San Diego and went to the San Diego zoo, a fun time for all of us.

Returning from San Diego, we had a hard time keeping up with all that others had planned for us. Several times people asked Darryl to speak about his illness. He enjoyed talking to the junior high kids in his brother Ray's youth group. As Darryl shared things God had brought into his life, they listened with rapt attention. They evidenced surprise that someone could show such contentment, even happiness, in such adverse circumstances. Darryl demonstrated a calm attitude as he told them that doctors had indicated he would probably die from his disease. This had an obvious sobering effect on that rambunctious group of young people. Darryl explained that he experienced God's peace because he knew Christ as his Savior. He looked forward to Heaven when he died, and this enabled him to remain calm and optimistic. He further challenged them that they could know that same peace, regardless of their circumstances, by trusting Christ as their Savior and Lord.

On June 15, Harvey and I celebrated our 25th wedding anniversary. Harvey's sister, Evelyn, graciously provided us with an incredible party, including a beautiful cake, to celebrate this milestone in our lives. Our older kids added an enduring treasure to this festive occasion.

Our 25th Wedding Celebration

Charlotte had taken a class in calligraphy during the previous school year. In that class, she produced, in beautiful calligraphic script, a 24" x 30" transcript of the scripture verses from Philippians 1 that Darryl had asked

Harvey to write for him the night he learned he had cancer. Inscribed on aged parchment paper, she had taken her professional-quality work a step further by enlisting an artistic friend of hers to draw a small, life-like, ink-dot picture of Darryl near the beginning of the scripture. Copied from Darryl's last school photo, this supplemented her already breathtaking production.

Char's masterpiece with framing by Ray and Tim

Ray and Tim also got involved by purchasing some ornately decorative framing material. Carefully cutting and joining their corners, that frame became the final touch in setting off Charlotte's painstaking and loving work of art. What an appropriate and appreciated gift at this juncture in our lives.

Soon after our exciting anniversary celebration, we packed up our car and borrowed trailer and headed over the mountains into northern California. Ray had a few days to spend with us before starting his summer job, so he followed us in his old '57 Chevy. Since it fit with his return route home, we first drove to Mt. Lassen National Park and were surprised to find snow remaining on the ground. This made it difficult to find a good—and dry—camping spot. In spite of the snow, we took several nice hikes around the area. We also enjoyed the bubbling pools found in the park even though they smelled like rotten eggs. When Ray left us to move on to his job in Colorado, we made our way toward a warmer place to camp, a beautiful California State Park, Patrick's Point.

Patrick's Point sits high on a coastal bluff in northern California looking out across the vast expanse of the Pacific Ocean. Here the beauty of mountains, forests and crashing waves intermingle. The mountains seem to blend right into the ocean. A multitude of hiking trails wind through giant trees often near the thundering waves below. Somehow, all of this beauty provided the illusion of separation from the clamoring world around. Relaxing, we were grateful that the burdens which had been weighing us down seemed lighter in this beautiful place.

One of the shaded trails near our campsite led to a long wooden stairway, a hundred steps or more, to the beautiful ocean below. No ordinary beach, an incredible variety of multi-colored pebbles cover the shore. It beckons rock hounds from near and far as they search for beautiful specimens of jasper, jade and agate, along with a great variety of other rocks and petrified wood. This huge, rock-strewn beach, constantly re-supplied by incoming giant waves, provided hours of relaxation and entertainment. We found an impressive variety of smooth sea-tumbled pebbles which we packed into our car to take home with us. At Patrick's Point, authorities make an exception to the usual rule of California State Parks. Both rocks and driftwood may be legally collected. Along with the pebbles collected, we also gathered some small but interesting pieces of driftwood to take back to Colorado with us.

We spent considerable time on the beach but not in the water. Posted signs warn that strong rip tides made swimming extremely dangerous. Even a good swimmer could be swept out to sea without any chance of being rescued. Huge rocks jutted into the ocean in many places. We savored the awe-inspiring sight of giant waves breaking on towering boulders, spraying to staggering heights, enhanced by the crystal clear blue sky beyond. We drank in the ever-changing beauty of this exotic area for several days before reluctantly starting our return trip to southern California. Even then, we continued to bask in the beauty of God's creation as we traveled the slower coastal route of Highway 1 for many miles southward.

After we returned the trailer to Harvey's parents, we headed north again to visit my mother and other family members in Turlock. Staying with my brother Wilbur felt like returning "home" to us. We had sold our memory-filled home to Wilbur and Vi when we moved to Colorado.

In spite of the many miles we had traveled, Darryl seemed to be doing well. He received his first required chemotherapy treatment at Children's Hospital in Los Angeles; now, in Turlock, he received another treatment from Dr. Frank Davis.

While in Turlock, Darryl was again asked to share his story, this time in a morning service at Monte Vista Chapel. God continued to challenge people as Darryl told how the Lord used his illness to glorify God. In an inexplicable way, Darryl seemed to carry a sense of mission and exhibited a commitment to use every day that God gave him to the fullest extent possible.

Chapter 14

INCREASING PRESSURE
AT HOME IN COLORADO

*H*aving completed the goals envisioned for our California trip, we started our journey home. We drove through without stopping to sleep for the night. The three children slept most of the way, but Harvey and I traded off driving and attempting to sleep. I always have difficulty sleeping while traveling, so I arrived home feeling exhausted.

We reached home at 9 AM and then slept for several hours. It took a few days to catch up, but the time away had been a tonic for all of us. Harvey, especially, had become extremely exhausted by a demanding schedule and benefited a great deal by this change of pace.

Darryl continued to improve. In fact, around the middle of July, he decided to take over his old paper route again. Doctors at the oncology clinic responded favorably to his idea and encouraged him to do it. His decision troubled Harvey and me. We remembered the difficulty of an early morning route. Even so, since he wanted to do it and his doctors concurred, we allowed him to try. To our surprise, he seemed to do quite well except for days following chemotherapy injections. These always made him sick, and he had to get a substitute for a day or two until his stomach felt settled.

In early August, doctors at the clinic decided to stop giving Darryl vincristine, one of his chemotherapy medications. We had noticed that he seemed to be stumbling as he walked. His doctors decided that this very strong drug might be affecting his leg tendons and could even cause irreversible damage.

Most of the family caught the flu in August; only Harvey escaped. Darryl, in his weakened condition, first acquired the bug and then shared it with the rest of the family. Unfortunately, Darryl's flu turned into pneumonia. This made it impossible for him to have scheduled chemotherapy injections. Just prior to his bout with the flu, he had decided on his own to give up his Rocky Mountain News route. He found the early morning hours and rigid schedule difficult to handle.

When he recovered from pneumonia, Darryl found a job at a pet store that had opened near our home. He enjoyed working with all the animals and developed a special interest in the numerous varieties of fish. Like many things in life, his new job soon developed some drawbacks. Another boy about the same age who worked at the pet shop delighted in teasing him. He tried everything possible to get Darryl to react. In particular, he loved to make fun of Darryl because he refused to get excited about girls. Determined to change Darryl's attitude, he tried to force Darryl to take addresses and phone numbers of some of his friends. He insisted that Darryl should call and ask one of them for a date. Exasperated, Darryl told him, "Look, I'm not old enough to go out with girls."

Upset, his fellow worker retorted, "Oh! So you're saying that I'm not old enough to go out with girls."

Darryl responded, "No, I said that I'm not mature enough yet to go out with girls." That seemed to end the discussion but Darryl continued to feel pressured by his fellow worker. One evening, as part of his assigned work, Darryl filled a tub with water in order to wash out the animal's feed dishes. For some reason the young store owner, egged on by Darryl's heckling fellow-worker, tried to throw him into the tub of water.

That night, I noticed Darryl's tension when he came home, so I gave him a back rub. As I rubbed his back I noticed several places where he had hemorrhaged under the skin. He told me about the attempted dunking episode, and I asked if this might have caused the marks on his body. He didn't think so. Then, several days later, Darryl found a lump on one of his ribs. With increasing concern, I reported this to the oncology clinic. They told me to bring Darryl in so they could examine him. Harvey planned to attend a conference in another state in a few days and I appreciated getting Darryl checked before Harvey left.

The doctor who examined Darryl concurred that the marks on his back must have come from the struggle as Darryl resisted being thrown into the tub, but he could not determine what caused the lump on his chest. He indicated that they would continue checking, watching for any relevant change. Needless to say, these developments increased my tension, leaving me with an uneasy feeling. Once again, God drew me back to His Word for comfort and encouragement. I appreciated those verses in Philippians 4 that continued to remind me that the peace of God *would* keep my heart and mind through Christ Jesus.

One night in October Darryl awakened with a terrible headache. I opened the couch hide-a-bed in the front room and brought him upstairs. Sitting by him, I rubbed his back through much of the night; this seemed to ease his extreme pain. I reported this to the clinic in the morning and the doctor on duty told me to bring Darryl in as quickly as possible. As soon as we arrived, one of the doctors performed a spinal tap and took a bone marrow sample. From these results, he shared the dire news. Cancer cells had invaded Darryl's brain.

Jolted by this new development, a daily flurry of new approaches confronted us as the oncology staff attempted to bring this added, unwelcome challenge under control. They started Darryl on another medication, methotrexate, to attempt to kill the now proliferating cancer cells. The following day they decided to do a biopsy on the growth on his left rib cage.

On Monday, Children's Hospital staff sent Darryl to another hospital where he could receive needed radiation treatment along with required spinal injections. Radiation treatments continued every weekday throughout the next three weeks, a total of fifteen treatments. This meant traveling daily to Denver from our home in Lakewood; it also meant spending hours each day at the hospital, constantly confronted with desperately ill and dying people in various stages of their battles with cancer.

I agonized as I spent time in this place and watched the devastation that cancer causes in so many lives. I could not help but think of the excruciating toll on health-care workers who live and work in the midst of all of this suffering day after day. As the end of this time of intensive treatment drew to a close, one of the doctors endeavored to say things on several occasions that would encourage me; but nothing took away the painful realization of Darryl's impossible condition. Once more, God provided a source of comfort, this time through the words of an old hymn, *Only Believe*:

> Fear not little flock, from the cross to the throne,
> From death into life He went for His own
> All power in earth, all power above,
> Is given to Him for the flock of His love.
>
> Chorus:
> Only believe, only believe;
> All things are possible, only believe;
> Only believe, only believe;
> All things are possible, only believe.
>
> Fear not little flock, He goeth ahead,
> Your shepherd selecteth the path you must tread;
> The waters of Marah He'll sweeten for thee-
> He drank all the bitter in Gethsemane.

Fear not little flock, whatever your lot;
He enters all rooms, the doors being shut,
He never forsakes, He never is gone—
So count on His presence in darkness and dawn.

With renewed commitment, which I realized could come only through God's enabling, I cast myself and our family on the Lord. He alone could provide the grace needed to take us through this ongoing storm called *CANCER*. One who has not experienced the trauma of cancer cannot fathom the difficulty involved. When Darryl went into remission I thought, "Maybe God will heal him." Then, when cancer cells reactivated, often in a new location as had happened now, or with increased intensity, I experienced that incredible resurgent pain.

Struggling anew with the possibility of losing Darryl, despair flooded every fiber of my being. Each time, I felt like I lost this beloved son all over again! Then my questioning spirit like a rushing torrent sought to overwhelm me, "Could I, did I, really believe that I could count on God to be with me and sweeten these bitter waters of Marah for me?"

The answer resounded through my being, "Yes! I could. *I must*." A verse of scripture that I memorized and that God used in my life at other times of difficulty came back to me. II Timothy 1:7 became a sustaining comfort: "For God hath not given us the spirit of fear; but of power, and of love, and of a sound mind." No matter what the final outcome, I must not give in to my fears. I must—I would—trust God, knowing that He does have my best interest in His heart. My God promised to sustain me in the midst of whatever storm might lie ahead.

What a relief to reach the point where the vigorous treatment brought Darryl's cancer into remission once more. Nonetheless, with this remission, Darryl faced a new problem. Chemotherapy received earlier had not caused his hair to fall out even though many experience such a reaction. Radiation produced different results. Staff at the clinic forewarned and urged us to buy a wig before it actually happened. They told us to do this because it would enable us to do a better job of matching the color of his hair and his hairstyle. A close match would make the use of a wig less obvious. Darryl did not like the style or hair length of available wigs, increasing the difficulty of finding a suitable match. Sure enough, one morning Darryl awoke to find hair all over his bed and much of the rest came out in clumps in his hands. Even though expected, this devastated him. Thankful for the advanced warning, we had the wig ready for him. Overnight, he became almost bald.

When Darryl went to school, kids noticed a difference in him. One boy decided to have some fun at his expense. Coming up behind Darryl, he yanked his wig off, exposing his bald head to the eyes of all the students nearby. In his fragile state, this embarrassed Darryl greatly.

Another humiliating experience occurred at our church. An older man entered the restroom at the same time as Darryl. This "saint" took him to task for having such long hair. By now Darryl had come to terms, to some extent, with his situation. Someone told us that, with a smile on his face, he removed his hair piece exposing his bald head. Still smiling, he said, "Sorry, this was the best I could find to cover this." Distressed by his thoughtless remarks and comprehending Darryl's problem, the man apologized for what he had said.

At the beginning of this renewed period of sickness and intense treatment, Darryl gave up his job at the pet shop. However, he persevered in raising betas (also called Siamese fighting fish) in his home aquarium. The male beta attracts the female by its beautiful fin and tail. That bright color enrages other males. Two male betas will attack each other and fight to the death. Consequently, a glass divider must separate male betas in the same tank. That does not prevent them from trying to reach their opponent. Charging each other, they butt into the dividing glass again and again. It amused us to watch their ferocious effort to destroy one another. We also found it amazing to watch the male beta carefully care for the fertilized eggs but then try to eat the newly hatched babies. Breeding these fish involved careful science in order for them to reach maturity. Darryl's project gave him a nice diversion and the rest of us amusing pleasure.

In these pressure filled days, Darryl spent more and more time on the phone with his friend and confidant, Aunt Helen. Despite the great difference in their ages, their affinity grew out of their mutual suffering. Without doubt, their frequent interaction nurtured in each of them a growing acceptance of the suffering God allowed them to experience. It continued to amaze us that a friendship bridging such disparate ages could be so comforting for both of them. Perhaps out of his ongoing contacts with Aunt Helen, Darryl commented to me one day, "You know Mom, I think that I'm beginning to understand old people. Being old is a lot like me. My body seems to be getting weaker and wasting away but I'm exactly the same person inside!"

We appreciated the fact that during these tough days in our lives, our two eldest children lived in the Denver area. Following her college graduation, Charlotte accepted the position of Women's Dorm Supervisor at Western. She also worked part-time in the school office and served as the school nurse. Since Ray now attended Denver Seminary, Western asked him to serve as Men's Dorm Supervisor. Dorm supervisor positions included housing along with meals in the student dining room.

Again this year, Tim returned home for the Christmas holidays, enabling our family to experience precious, memory-filled hours together. As expected, those days passed too fast, and Tim had to return to complete his senior year at Biola.

Chapter 15

I'D RATHER BE WITH JESUS

*J*anuary 5 followed soon after those wonderful days of Christmas family time. I would never forget that just a year before, on Darryl's fourteenth birthday, our world changed forever. On that day Dr. Kurtz communicated the devastating word that Darryl had only one or two months to live. But God! He gave us another full year to enjoy Darryl's presence. On his fifteenth birthday which we had thought we would never celebrate with him, he had an appointment at the clinic. On the way home I asked him, "Well Darryl, you've had a year of life that no one expected you to have. How do you feel about that?"

Although his answer showed a perspective on life that all of us should have, I found it hard to accept and it caused pain like a sword piercing through my heart. Darryl responded, "Mom, I love our home, and I love you and Dad; but I'd rather be with Jesus."

I don't know what I expected, but I didn't anticipate the answer he gave. My whole being cried out, "No! We want you here with us." God summoned him in a way I didn't understand. Darryl's depth of perception and his love for his Lord reached beyond my ability to grasp or accept at that time.

In the second week of February, Darryl's health took a sudden turn for the worse. Examining him, his doctors told me they didn't know where his illness would go. They suggested that he may have developed a tumor on his liver, reacted to medication, or contracted infectious hepatitis. His skin turned yellow. Even when the yellow color of his skin began to fade, they decided he must have infectious hepatitis in spite of inconclusive blood tests. They told him to stay out of school for an additional three weeks and return to the clinic for weekly tests. When he felt better and his appetite returned, we concluded that this crisis had passed.

A friend provided our family with tuition to attend a Basic Youth Conflicts Seminar in Kansas in February. Darryl had anticipated going with us, but his jaundiced condition prevented him. Charlotte offered to stay with him. She had attended the seminar in Los Angeles the previous year, so insisted that we go. She told us she would take care of Darryl as well as her two younger sisters. We realized later the great benefit of getting away for a while and distancing ourselves from the day-to-day crises which defined our lives.

A day or two into the seminar, Charlotte called and told us that the doctors had concluded that Darryl's cancer had traveled to his liver. This confirmed the real reason for his yellow skin. She told us that Darryl itched so badly it nearly drove him crazy.

We told Charlotte we would return home immediately. She discouraged us from that and urged us to complete the seminar. Although difficult, we consented. We found it hard to focus on the challenging material presented after receiving her report, but God continued to minister to us through the words spoken.

As it turned out, ongoing events nearly overwhelmed Charlotte. She spent two entire days with Darryl at the clinic. She also took him to the hospital for a second round of radiation treatments. The clinic personnel injected radioactive dye into his veins and then took x-rays over a period of an hour in order to identify the problem in his liver. A swollen lymph node blocked his bile duct. At the same time, the intense radiation caused him to develop a fever. His doctors warned of possible soreness developing in the area of his abdomen where they focused the high-powered machine. They gave Charlotte some salve, instructing her to cover the affected area when it hurt.

Adding to Charlotte's burden, Susan got the flu and ran a high fever. Then the furnace broke. Someone from Western Bible Institute volunteered to repair it. It broke again. Her helpful Samaritan returned to repair it a second time, but on two different days she and her siblings had to get along without heat during the freezing temperatures of a Colorado February. Had we known all Charlotte faced we would have returned home despite her protests. But in her capable way, she kept on top of those pressurized days and allowed us to complete the seminar.

When we returned to Lakewood, I took Darryl to his next regularly scheduled appointment at Children's Hospital. One of the doctors explained the ongoing radiation treatments Darryl was now receiving at the Presbyterian Medical Center. They used a linear accelerator called the *LINAC*, a piece of equipment new to the Denver area. This high-powered machine concentrated 4 million volts of power on a small square on Darryl's abdomen over his liver. Each high intensity treatment lasted only a short time. A pamphlet designed to explain to lay-people the wonders of this new equipment stated that fiberglass panels, finished in light green, made the machine very attractive. I scorned the idea that a machine which seemed so threatening could be considered attractive.

On March 6, we received a further disheartening report following Darryl's bone marrow test. Lab technicians found leukemic cells in his blood and in his bone marrow sample. Hearing that Darryl had now developed acute lymphocytic leukemia, along with his lymphosarcoma, I recalled that early in Darryl's illness Dr. Holton had told me that lymphosarcoma usually developed into leukemia. How I had hoped it wouldn't come to this!

I found it hard to stay positive. The oncology team working with Darryl decided that he needed to continue with radiation. They also treated him again with all four of the drugs which they gave when they first diagnosed him with cancer. They had not injected him with cytoxan and vincristine for several months, but his doctors felt that returning him to the full treatment provided the greatest potential for hitting this formidable cancer. We only hoped and prayed that their calculation proved true. We recalled the warning given us when Darryl began receiving treatment. All current, available medications still remained in an early, experimental stage. These new medications provided hope but no one knew potential final results.

The strain of more than a year of our roller coaster existence—hope followed by despair, followed by renewed hope—took its toll. Now, going with Darryl to this latest series of radiation treatments at Presbyterian Hospital turned into one of the hardest experiences that I faced as a mother. Every patient waiting for treatment looked like death warmed over.

Although I had ached to see so many sick children in the waiting room at the oncology clinic at Children's Hospital, I had learned to cope with that particular setting. As parents, we visited and got to know each other as we discussed our children's individual situations. Of course, it hurt as I observed some child with face puffing up who appeared sicker with each visit. Then, his or her parent—and the child—no longer came, and I could only surmise what had happened.

I had difficulty experiencing that repeated, ongoing scenario at the oncology clinic but this new setting at Presbyterian Hospital carried me exponentially beyond my ability to deal with the hurt. I tried to steel myself against thinking about all of this but pushed myself into overload during these cancer-fighting days.

The date for teaching some classes on *Children and the Christian Home* at Western Bible Institute which I had earlier committed to came in the midst of this latest intense episode. I know that I managed to teach these classes, while keeping up with Darryl's radiation treatments and increased oncology clinic appointments, only because God enabled me to do so.

After multiplied sessions on the linear accelerator machine, along with chemotherapy, Darryl entered another period of remission. By the end of

March, he felt great and acted like our happy, challenging young son again. Relief flooded my being as I experienced renewed hope for Darryl's health.

In times of deep distress, God often provided special encouragement. In this same month, we received some gratifying news from California. Tim called to announce his engagement to Mary Murphy. Our earlier contacts with Mary led us to believe she would make a wonderful wife for Tim.

It did not surprise me that I often struggled to get everything on my agenda completed. In addition to transporting Darryl to his appointments, I also had to take the girls to the doctor when they got sick which happened more often than we desired. Furthermore, I took Faith to her piano lesson each week. When Harvey figured out our income tax, I gained insight into part of my problem. The IRS allowed us to deduct mileage for medical appointments, so we kept careful records of all those trips. He calculated that we had traveled 2,200 miles for medical appointments alone in the past year.

Jefferson County School District now provided a home teacher because Darryl's illness resulted in many absences. When his teacher started this assignment in our home, she planned to come for only a few weeks—until Darryl caught up with missed classroom work. Darryl liked Mrs. Barnett and flourished under her teaching. He found this much easier than the daily classroom pressure he experienced the previous year, so was glad when school authorities extended her assignment to serve as his teacher.

Having this home teacher also freed Darryl to do some other things that he enjoyed. Irises bloomed in our yard in the spring. With his eye for beauty, Darryl picked a couple of those irises and placed them in a vase on the dining room table. He then proceeded to draw one of them. Since the result pleased him, he enclosed his finished picture in this letter to Aunt Helen:

Dear Aunt Helen,

Thought I'd send a little something to cheer ya. We have some irises on the dining room table, so I decided to draw one.

When I got finished I thought it might be something you might like, so I sent it to you.

Isn't it neat to know that pretty soon we get to see Jesus, who is more glorious than the prettiest iris?

Love in Christ,

Darryl

Darryl's longing to be with Jesus evidenced itself in the things he wrote as well as in his speech. He found great delight in sharing those feelings with his special soul-mate. Their interaction helped both of them.

During May, another doctor joined the staff that cared for Darryl at the oncology clinic. As Dr. Baum entered the examining room one day, he held up his fingers forming a "V" sign for peace. Without a moment's hesitation, Darryl, holding up a closed fist with one finger pointing skyward, said, "Dr. Baum why don't you give this sign instead?"

"What does that mean?" Dr. Baum queried.

"That's the sign the Jesus People make. Hippies, who have found Christ as their Savior, let others know that they belong to Jesus by pointing up to heaven toward Him." Needless to say, Dr. Baum did not quite know what to say to this friendly, but out-spoken, patient he had just acquired.

In mid-May, our fragile world crashed in on us again. It looked as if our planned trip to Tim's graduation in California had to be placed on hold. What a relentless foe we continued to fight! Lab results showed leukemia cells once more invaded Darryl's blood and bone marrow. His doctors began giving him another new experimental drug called daunomycin. After receiving the last injection in this series, doctors warned me that this medication literally knocked out all of Darryl's white blood cells, making him vulnerable to any disease that came along. They cautioned that he had nothing left to fight infection until his good white cells began to come back. We needed to keep him away from crowds of any kind as well as avoid anyone with a cold or flu.

Returning home from the clinic, I followed the instructions given me. I cleaned the whole house and scrubbed down the bathrooms. I sprayed with Lysol, and we all gargled with Scope several times a day. If Darryl avoided infection for four days, we could assume he had passed through the period of critical danger.

Dr. Baum then added the further somber possibility that if this drug did not take away the leukemia cells he could do nothing more for him. But Darryl's bone marrow sample taken the following week revealed that the medicine had indeed eradicated the leukemic cells at that time and good white cells began to multiply. Darryl entered remission for the fourth time.

Despite this continuing roller coaster existence, doctors encouraged us to proceed with plans to attend Tim's graduation. We made the arduous trip to California, again driving the whole distance without stopping to sleep. This year Darryl's presence made our car a happier place. With his home school teacher, Darryl had completed his school work early enough to travel with us. Sure enough, he kept Faith and Susan in much better spirits.

Harvey's parents provided a trip to Disneyland, a highlight of this journey to southern California. Although a long and involved day, we all enjoyed a great time. Even Harvey and I appreciated some of the "tamer" rides, and we delighted in the special family time together. It pleased us to see Darryl enjoy this day; yet, we felt apprehensive as he insisted on taking advantage of all the exhilarating opportunities.

We did not plan to spend as much time in California this year, but after Tim's graduation we still included a visit to my mother and brother in Turlock. Traveling north, we stopped to eat at a park in Fresno; it contained a zoo and some amusement rides. Kids being kids, they again begged, and we let them go on several of the whirligigs. Darryl went with his sisters but did not feel well afterward.

We completed our trip to Turlock, and Darryl continued to feel sick. I wondered if going on some of those wilder rides, following our earlier time at Disneyland, did something that negatively impacted his body. We only stayed a day or two in Turlock feeling an urgency to get Darryl back home and into contact with his doctors.

His condition didn't improve. To make the trip back to Colorado easier for him, we decided to stop at a motel in northern Nevada. He continued to feel sick. I felt apprehensive and anxious to get him back for a check-up at the oncology clinic. I watched his health deteriorate before my eyes.

Chapter 16

DON'T CALL ME POOR!

We called the clinic as soon as we got home. After running several tests and examining Darryl, clinic personnel concluded that the daunomycin no longer helped him. They put him back on methotrexate, a medicine given him before Christmas. Since this medicine resulted in remission earlier, they hoped it might work again.

This time, however, Darryl developed huge sores in his mouth. After further checking, his doctors discovered the medication had turned his whole alimentary canal into an open sore from his mouth through his bowels. They admitted him to Children's Hospital, hoping to clear up this excruciating condition. My mind continued to mull over the question, "Why did this medicine affect him like this now when it hadn't bothered him before?"

They put him on a diet of jello and fluids. As I sat beside his bed I considered the ache I felt with one canker sore in my mouth. My mind churned out the question, "How must Darryl feel with the equivalent of a huge canker sore extending through his whole body?" Once again, my heart quaked at this unbelievable turn of events.

Hurting for Darryl as he thought of the pain he must be experiencing, Harvey sat by his bed the next day and placed his hand on Darryl's leg. Patting his leg, Harvey said, "Poor Darryl."

Turning a little so he could look up into his dad's face a near-smile formed as Darryl said, "Don't call me poor, Dad. If this is what God has planned for me just now, this is the very best thing that could be happening to me."

Dr. Baum came into Darryl's hospital room on a rainy day to check on him. Making conversation, he said, "Well, Darryl, you brought the rain today." As he checked Darryl the following sunshiny day, Dr. Baum said, "Well, Darryl, you brought the sunshine today."

Without a pause, Darryl responded, "Dr. Baum, yesterday you said that I brought the rain. Today you said that I brought the sunshine. Dr. Baum, God brings the rain, and it is God who brings the sunshine."

Thoughtfully, looking out the window at the glorious sunshine and then looking back at Darryl, Dr. Baum said, "You think a lot about God, don't you?"

"Yes," Darryl answered quietly.

"Darryl, you believe in God, don't you?"

Without a moment's hesitation, Darryl responded, "Yes, I do." To Darryl, the reality of God and his relationship to God were so genuine that a conversation such as this was as natural as breathing.

On another day, our friend and fellow teacher with Harvey at Western Bible Institute, Bill Boyd, went to visit Darryl at the hospital. Sensing Darryl's joyful and triumphant spirit in spite of his circumstances, Bill said, "Darryl, you're incredible."

Darryl's near-automatic, quick counter caught Bill by surprise, "No, Bill, I'm not incredible. I just have an incredible God living in me."

Once again, it amazed us to see how God spoke about issues that paralleled events in Darryl's life through his good friend and pen-pal, Aunt Helen. She sent him a card which included a poem by Edith Lillian Young. It contained a message which she shared with Darryl because it had spoken to her:

A Child of the King

Poor, of course not! Why, how could I be,
When Christ the King is taking care of me?

Tired? Sometimes—yes, more than tired; but then,
I know a place where I can rest again!

Lonely? Ah! Well I know the aching blight;
But now, I've Jesus with me day and night.

Burdens? I have them, oft they press me sore.
And then, I lean the harder, trust the more.

Worthy? Ah no! The marvel of it is
That I should know such boundless love as His!

As so, I'm rich with Christ! I am "joint heir."
Since He once stooped my poverty to share.

Aunt Helen's card included a personal note that said, "I'm praying that God's will be done—I miss your happy voice—I love you so very much."

During this hospital stay I had an interesting exchange with some of Darryl's doctors. One of them called me out of his room. Several doctors had gathered and one of them asked, "Doesn't Darryl say anything to you?"

Not understanding just what he meant, I responded that Darryl communicated with me quite well. I then added that he had told me a few days before that he felt uncomfortable to have a woman doctor. A new woman doctor from the Philippines recently joined the staff, and Darryl expressed embarrassment when she examined him. His difficulty understanding her English added to his awkward feelings.

The questioning doctor shot back, "No, we don't mean about things like that. Doesn't he complain about pain? He should be having insurmountable pain right now."

When I responded, "No, he hasn't been complaining about pain at all," those gathered doctors looked at each other confounded by my response. One by one, they walked away shaking their heads.

Later, one of these incredulous doctors explained that they expected Darryl to experience severe pain at this point. No doubt, they remembered that we had refused to have Darryl enter their psychological hypnosis program. It puzzled them that instead of complaining of excruciating pain, he didn't even mention it. As I observed their confounded response, God reminded me again of Psalm 41:3. "The Lord will strengthen him upon his bed of languishing; thou wilt make all his bed in his sickness." I had no answer except that God was doing this for Darryl. He was meeting his needs and ministered to him at this crucial time. We had trusted Him with Darryl's pain. Now, God either gave him strength to handle it or, perhaps, kept him from it. God affirmed His faithfulness.

Darryl's physical condition showed no improvement. Several doctors asked me to join them in one of their offices. I observed somber looks on their faces. They informed me that they planned to take Darryl off of all medication. They had exhausted every form of treatment and further medication would do no good. As soon as the sores in Darryl's mouth healed, he could go home.

Leaving the doctor's office, I again yearned with the hope that God may still choose to heal Darryl. Had God waited until doctors removed all medications to heal him? Is this what would bring glory to God?

At the same time, my mind continued to wrestle with the sobering reality of what the doctor had said. In the midst of my emotional turmoil, God began to give peace—a peace that could not be explained as any normal, human reaction. Once again, I committed the coming days to God. He held Darryl's future in His loving, all-knowing and wise hands. I must trust Him as He, alone, made the decision whether to heal Darryl or to take him to heaven.

We took Darryl home the third week in July. The doctors released him because the sores in his mouth had healed. We didn't give him an upstairs bedroom this time, feeling that he would rest better in the familiar surroundings of his basement bedroom. At the same time, we recognized his weakened condition and didn't want to leave him isolated if he needed assistance. Harvey installed a buzzer in Darryl's room that rang upstairs when he needed something. He greatly appreciated staying in the familiar surroundings of his own room.

As I spent time with Darryl, I shared with him about the time when I felt God led me to pray for his healing. Given some of the things that Darryl had told us and others about his desire to be with Jesus, I guess it shouldn't have surprised me that this word did not overly excite him.

I also told him of the pressure doctors at the clinic had placed on us to enter him into a class to train him to respond to psychological hypnosis. I explained that they felt this would help control the pain he would experience in the future. When I told him that we had refused this training for him in spite of intense pressure from the oncology staff, he responded without any hesitation, "Oh, Mother, I'm so glad you didn't let them force me into a class like that." He then went on to tell me that when the doctors took his bone marrow, an intensely painful experience, he just thought about Jesus dying on the cross and how much pain Jesus went through for him. "Mom," he went on, "if you would have let the doctors do this to me, you would have robbed me of a deep spiritual experience. I'm so glad that you didn't let them do it." Even then, he never complained about pain, and I didn't ask him. Somehow, I felt that I had to leave those secrets between him and God.

We saw no change in Darryl's physical condition throughout the month of July. He continued in bed most of the time; nevertheless, he still exhibited a lot of determination. As my birthday approached on the 29th of July, he shocked me by suggesting, "Mom, why don't we go on a picnic to celebrate your birthday?" Surprised, I responded, "Why Darryl, how can you go on a picnic when it's hard for you to even sit up?"

Darryl had it all planned out. "Just bring along a camp cot," he replied, "and I'll lie down beside our picnic table."

Darryl on his camp cot as we picnic on my birthday
at one of our favorite spots in the mountains

Darryl loved the mountains and missed the wonderful times he and his dad had spent hiking together. He also missed the times we as a family had camped together in those mountains. Now, since he longed once more to get up into some of that God-ordained grandeur, we decided to honor his wish. We prepared a picnic lunch and headed thirty miles up into the Rockies to one of our favorite places beside a small stream.

Darryl welcomed the ride and experienced supreme pleasure in seeing God's great and beautiful outdoors. He loved the beauty and awe-inspiring splendor of the Rocky Mountains. We had a delightful time together even though Darryl could only lie down on his cot. It amazed us to see Darryl evidence and share an infectious joy. He lived life to the fullest in spite of any physical limitation that came his way. His exuberant participation made this picnic a special and memorable time for all of us.

Harvey had a scheduled week-long speaking engagement at a youth camp in southwestern Colorado near Four Corners and he planned to leave the following day. He had reservations about going since Darryl's physical strength continued to diminish. Actually, Darryl had wanted to go with his dad to this camp and had received permission from the camp director to go. He kept hoping to go, but in the end acknowledged that he did not have the strength to make the trip. With my encouragement, Harvey decided that he himself should go since he had made a commitment to the camp.

To pacify the fact of his dad being gone that night and thinking about missing the camp, Darryl asked Ray to sleep out on the lawn with him. Ray replied that he would love to. The girls heard about these plans and decided to join them. They all carried out quilts and other sleeping gear to the back lawn. I even joined them for a while. What a beautiful night! The stars twinkled in their splendor above us. At some time during the night, Darryl decided to move to the comfort of his own bed and made his way back to his room. His siblings finished their "campout" without him.

On Thursday afternoon I went into Darryl's room and sat on his bed. I held his hand as we talked. It startled me to find an apparent rapid pulse and I asked Charlotte to check it for me. As she grasped his wrist, a puzzled look spread across her face, "You're right, Mom. I think you need to contact the oncology clinic immediately."

When I called the clinic, they told me to bring Darryl to the hospital. They wasted no time in admitting him and began a battery of tests. Charlotte and I went home and made supper since clinic rules didn't allow us to stay with Darryl during his tests. We returned to the hospital after supper and took Faith and Susan with us. We didn't usually take them along but Char was eager to return to the hospital and Ray had to go to work. I had no one else to watch them and I couldn't leave them home alone. Faith and Susan were under 12 years old but the hospital staff bent the rules and allowed them to enter Darryl's room through the clinic area of the hospital. Darryl was lethargic but did not appear to feel too bad. We stayed with him until visiting hours ended. We returned home thankful that the girls had the opportunity to see him.

When I called Children's Hospital early the next morning they said, "Mrs. Stranske, Darryl's condition is very grave!"

With this disquieting news, I realized that I needed to contact Harvey. The camp he was at was located in an isolated forest area and had no phone service. The camp director had instructed me to call the forest ranger stationed near the national forest entrance if I needed to get a message to Harvey. I succeeded in contacting the ranger and asked him to convey the message to Harvey that his son's situation had turned critical. He needed to return home as quickly as possible. The ranger assured me that he would deliver my message.

Unknown to me, Harvey had just spent time in the hospital. Awakened in the middle of the night with acute abdominal pain like he had experienced before, Harvey recognized this as another kidney stone attack. He tried to avoid bothering others in the middle of the night and so he lay in bed for several hours writhing in pain. By 4:30 in the morning, his agony pushed him to call for help. Without delay, the camp director arranged for a staff member to drive Harvey to the hospital in Durango.

Harvey experienced uncontrollable pain for most of the day in the hospital on Tuesday. Since morphine provided no relief, the hospital staff insisted that he needed urgent surgery. They pressed him to allow them to inform me, but Harvey refused to let them call. He explained that he didn't want to burden me because of our son's critical condition. Finally, late in the afternoon the kidney stone passed. Harvey was exhausted but free from his excruciating pain. He still felt weak, but they released him from the hospital the following morning. He couldn't fulfill his speaking responsibility that evening, but he felt better after getting a good night's sleep.

A strange thing happened as Harvey prayed and thought about his message for Thursday evening. He had planned to share Darryl's story with this group of eager young people on Friday—the last day of the camp. In that final message, Harvey wanted to focus on the importance of submission to the will of God regardless of the circumstances God allows into our lives. For some reason, Harvey felt an urgency to use the material planned for Friday evening on Thursday.

He sensed God moving in a powerful way in the lives of those young people as he spoke that evening. Later on, several of the young people in that service let Harvey know that they made a commitment to the Lord that led them to attend Western Bible Institute and pursue a life of Christian service. As Harvey sank into a deep sleep that night, he recognized that he did not know what he would speak about Friday evening. Yet he felt satisfied in believing that he had done what God wanted him to do.

The thoughtful forest ranger recognized the urgency of the message which I asked him to convey to Harvey on Friday morning and lost no time in making his way to the camp. When Harvey received word of Darryl's deteriorating condition, he understood why God had led him to use his concluding message the night before. Although he still felt weak, he quickly packed and began the 400-mile trip home, stopping at the ranger station long enough to phone and let me know that he had started on his way.

Meanwhile, in a daze, I made breakfast for the family and prepared to go to Children's Hospital. Since Ray worked evenings—he got off at 11:00 PM—he could stay with the girls during the morning hours. I gasped as I walked into Darryl's room. The change that had occurred overnight astounded me. I remembered, with gratefulness, the kindness of hospital staff in allowing our young girls to visit him the night before. Today, Darryl lay flat on his back with his eyes closed. I spoke to him but received only a weak response. He did not open his eyes. Charlotte had come to the hospital with me, and I asked her to print out Philippians 4:7 on a little chalkboard hanging on the wall of Darryl's room. "And the peace of God which passeth all understanding shall keep your hearts and minds through Christ Jesus." In light of what Darryl had done with scripture verses earlier, it seemed fitting that we should affirm to anyone coming into the room that our God was still in control. We felt God sustaining us through this difficult time and giving us His peace. Furthermore, having God's promise on the chalkboard helped comfort our aching hearts.

That afternoon Dr. Baum came in to see Darryl. As he spoke to Darryl in his pleasant, joking manner, Darryl responded by giving him a smile of recognition. I sat by his bed all day long, but returned home for a quick supper. Harvey arrived home at 6:30 PM, exhausted from his long journey.

Harvey and I returned to the hospital at 7:30 PM. As Harvey leaned over the bed he said, "Hello, Darryl."

Without opening his eyes, Darryl responded in a weak voice, "Hi, Dad."

We sat together beside his bed throughout the evening, not saying much, but agonizing inside. At around 9:30, Darryl tried to say something. Becoming quite excited, he seemed to stammer, "That's the place where Jesus . . . . That's the place where Jesus . . . ." He just couldn't finish his sentence.

Pausing briefly, Darryl spoke again, "That's the place where He . . . . That's the place where He . . . ." As before, he couldn't finish his sentence. Both Harvey and I felt sure that we stood in the presence of a glimpse beyond this earthly life, convinced that Darryl saw the gates of heaven opening for him, with the Lord Jesus welcoming him home. The grandeur of what he saw must have been simply too great to express.

Then Darryl spoke again in a very clear voice, "Jesus died on the cross for my sins and for your sins."

Bending over his bed and grasping his arm, Harvey asked, "Are you going to see Jesus?"

Without a moment's hesitation Darryl responded with great confidence, "I'm going to see Him."

Hearing Darryl speak, one of the nurses decided to quell his restlessness. Coming in as we listened intently to hear if he would speak further, she gave him an injection. This saddened me. After the injection, he no longer spoke. In fact, his breathing became very heavy. Looking at Darryl with obvious compassion, the nurse said, "You know, at this point, he could slip into a coma and live on for weeks or he could die very soon."

As we became aware that we could no longer interact with Darryl, both of us recognized our overwhelming exhaustion. I had spent the long emotional day here at Darryl's bedside; Harvey, already weakened by his bout with kidney stones, had driven from Durango before coming to the hospital with me. Seeing our exhaustion, one of the nurses urged us to try to get some sleep. With Darryl now in a deep sleep, and in light of the suggestion that he might continue in a coma for weeks, we reluctantly concurred that this might be wise. She readied cots for us several doors away from Darryl's room. We went in to lie down with some reservation. We heard Darryl's labored breathing from that nearby room—a difficult experience to say the least. We didn't think we could sleep but, apparently, we did.

Just before midnight, the nurse knocked at the door and informed us that Darryl had died. We had chosen to rest under the assumption that Darryl may remain in a coma for days. Now we grieved that he had slipped into God's presence without us by his side. Unbelievably, Darryl's request to celebrate my birthday at our favorite picnic place had come only six days before.

Exhausted, we started to go home at 1:00 AM, but the nurse told us we needed to wait until Dr. Baum arrived at the hospital to talk to us. When Dr. Baum arrived about a half hour later he asked us to sit down with him in his office. He began, "You know we've sort of felt during the last month or two that, even though we were the ones that were supposed to be taking care of Darryl, he was really the one that was taking care of us. In fact, I am almost jealous of someone who can go so easily."

Harvey replied, "You know Dr. Baum, there is a reason why Darryl went so easily. He had received Jesus Christ as his Savior. Darryl loved Jesus and wanted to be with Him. So Darryl viewed dying as a transition to a better place. He looked forward to the opportunity to join his Savior, the one whom he had known and loved for much of his life. And as Darryl shared with you, Dr. Baum, you are not precluded from experiencing the same peace that Darryl found."

Dr. Baum's eyes fell as he responded, "I know I'm not exempt." This dear Jewish doctor had had others who belonged to Jesus die while under his care. A little girl of three years had stolen Dr. Baum's heart as he had treated her. A few weeks earlier she sat on his lap and told him, "You know, Jesus can help me."

Dr. Baum acknowledged to her, "Yes, and that makes two of us Jews who will help you." Soon after, this little girl contracted pneumonia and died because she lacked immunity due to the cancer drugs. Feeling great sorrow in losing her this way, Dr. Baum grieved right along with her parents. A short time later, her parents found a single red rose on her tiny grave; they later discovered that Dr. Baum had visited the gravesite and placed it there.

We appreciated the caring doctors who, even when daily confronted with such pain, misery and loss, retained the capacity for great love and compassion. We observed that many of these doctors, in their caring humanness, became attached to the children with whom they worked. They too suffered as these children, one after another, died.

After completing our early morning talk with Dr. Baum, we drove through the deserted streets of Denver to our home in Lakewood. Those streets reflected the emptiness that Harvey and I felt inside as we realized we would never again have the opportunity of enjoying a face-to-face chat with our vibrant, challenging son here on this earth. He truly had been a treasure, a special loan from God for these few years. Even in our grief, we recognized the richness of the gift God had privileged us to enjoy. Darryl had taught us so very much; but now he reached the pinnacle of his desire. He dwelt in the presence of his beloved Lord Jesus. I envisioned him beaming with that great, big, infectious smile as Christ greeted him, "Well done, son. You have been a good and faithful servant."

Chapter 17

A CONTINUING LEGACY HE
BEING DEAD YET SPEAKETH

After Darryl died, we wanted to show our appreciation to the hospital staff who had worked with him through his long illness. We concluded that nothing better reflected the life Darryl lived before them than God's Word, so we purchased a Living Bible for each of these special people who had become our friends in the oncology department. Charlotte personalized each Bible in a beautiful, calligraphic script.

Thank you notes received reflected the profound spiritual impact Darryl's life and death had made. The nurse who primarily cared for Darryl during his weekly visits to the clinic seemed to sum up the feeling of many. She stated, "His unshakable faith in God is something we can all learn from."

Recognizing the special relationship that the girl in the hematology department had developed with Darryl, we gave Lori Chesler Darryl's personal copies of the four Gospels. Darryl had enjoyed his individually bound copies of Matthew, Mark, Luke and John in the Living Bible version, and we felt that Lori would profit by them. Expressing her gratitude, Lori thanked us for "giving [her] the opportunity to share the deep peace through faith in Jesus Christ, which Darryl knew. It is one of the most meaningful things that anyone has ever done for me . . . ."

Some time later, Lori came over to our home and we shared how Jesus Christ had died for her. As we talked with Lori, she made the decision to accept Him as her Savior and left our home that night as a newborn child of God. She went to college in Greeley, Colorado that fall. From there she wrote, ". . . The Lord has answered my prayers and I know he will see me through when times get rough." Lori shared with us that she had begun going to church and had enrolled in a Navigator's Bible study group. We took pleasure in seeing God work in her life.

We received letters from other caregivers who had contact with Darryl. A nurse at Porter's hospital wrote how the nursing staff had all grown "to love Darryl in his short stay at Porters . . . . His love for the Savior just radiated all over."

Several staff members at Darryl's school, Dunstan Junior High, spoke highly of their interaction with Darryl. One teacher wrote, "I have never met anyone with his wisdom, honesty, and sincerity."

Bob Baker, Darryl's principal, wrote:

> The last time Darryl came to school was a pleasant sharing time for the two of us. His attitude, as well as always, was one of confidence and relaxation, knowing he was accepting God's will for whatever transpired . . . .

Nancy Woolnough, who worked at HCJB, in Quito, Ecuador, wrote to us again:

> I just want to thank you for remembering me and sending along the word about Darryl's terrific testimony and life and home going.
>
> I did use his interview with Harvey last year, and now I'll use this material too, for our radio audience. It makes us old timers ashamed.

A letter from my sister, Eldora Schwab, serving as a missionary in Japan, stated:

> Darryl's life down here was just a brief moment in the light of eternity—and yet I'm sure we'll never fully know, until we join him in heaven, just how many lives have been touched and turned toward the Lord Jesus because of his constant, loving confidence in Him, and his enthusiastic desire that others know the Lord, too.

Rocky Mountain News announced Darryl's death and reprinted the picture they had used with the article printed a year before. A few days later, the reporter who had visited us in our home and interviewed Darryl for that story, wrote an article, "A Lesson in Young Courage," on the op-ed page of the News:

> It isn't fun to be sent out to interview somebody who knows he's going to die. It doesn't help any if the somebody in question is 14 years old. Or if he's bright, talented and has plenty of ideas about what to do when he grows up yet knows he'll probably never get to grow up.
>
> Stories like that aren't fun to write, but they get written. For one thing they're part of the human drama, close enough to life's core to provide raw material for any serious writer.
>
> Photographer, Mel Scheiltz, and I were sent to the Lakewood residence of Mr. and Mrs. Harvey Stranske nearly 19 months ago to cover just such a story. I went with much anxiety, but what I found wasn't what I expected at all.
>
> Inside the house we found smiling faces and an open candid willingness—even eagerness—to tell the whole story. The smiles weren't the kind you see at a funeral with tears sneaking around the edges, but general relaxed expressions of inner peace.
>
> The Stranskes proved to be a remarkable family whose members professed deep religious convictions and had the quiet

courage to live by them. Phrases I'd heard long ago in Sunday School and had later rejected because I heard them mouthed by hypocrites—came alive here and made sense.

Darryl joined his parents and let us know quickly that nobody was keeping any secrets from him. When hard questions hesitated on my tongue, he eased me through with rare poise for a boy in early adolescence.

How do you ask a boy if he's ready to put his faith on the line, or whether he's prepared himself for a moment of truth that terrifies learned men of many times his age? He smiled and stated it very simply: that moment was near and he'd faced it with his eyes open.

Last Sunday I looked at Darryl's smiling picture in the paper, along with the inevitable story that said that his fight with cancer was over. It brought back the twinge that came that January day when Mel took the photo and I realized it would be filed away for just this use, at the point when Darryl's time ran out.

Darryl however, never saw it as time running out. Rather he looked forward to a walk through a door to another place. He believed this I'm sure with absolute conviction. In the process he overcame fear—and earned my deep respect.

And so I fought the urge to shed tears this week and reminded myself that if anybody I'd met could teach me something, it was this brave smiling young man.

Whatever it is you've found on the other side of that door, Darryl, may God bless you.[7]

A week or so before Darryl died, I wrote a letter to the Haven of Rest. They aired their daily radio broadcast on a network across the U.S., as well as on missionary radio stations around the world. They had a special day of prayer each August and asked that listeners send requests to be included for prayer on that day. Responding to their request, I sent a copy of the

---

[7] Article written by Alan Cunningham of the *Rocky Mountain News* owned by Scripps Media, Inc. Used by permission.

original article published in the Rocky Mountain News, along with other information about Darryl. I requested that they join us in praying for him.

They wrote a letter on August 2 to tell us they were praying for Darryl. This letter reached us a day or two after he died. In the difficult days following Darryl's home going, I neglected to write and tell them of his death. In another letter, dated August 17, they wrote to let us know that they would like to air a program about Darryl on October 3. Having read the material sent to them, they felt that it would exalt the Lord to tell his story. I wrote back, telling them that Darryl had now met his Savior face-to-face. Their immediate response indicated that they still desired to release a broadcast about Darryl on the scheduled date—if that would be acceptable to us. We gladly agreed to their request.

When we listened to their broadcast on the designated day, it amazed us to hear the superb job they had done. As usual, they blended music with carefully prepared commentary. The message conveyed on the program personally comforted me. We copied it and I listened to it over and over again. In a clear, concise way, the program told of the gift of salvation. Humbled, we recognized that by reason of Darryl's life and death, millions heard the message of God's love.

A fellow missionary from Sudan, Olive Rawn, heard the Haven of Rest program featuring Darryl in her new field of ministry, the Congo. She regularly listened to the Haven of Rest over the missionary short wave radio station, ELWA, in Liberia, a ministry of the Sudan Interior Mission. Olive sent word concerning this program and Darryl's death to many of our friends in several other countries in Africa.

Bill Boyd, the Western Bible Institute instructor whom Darryl had told about his "incredible God," wrote and shared the obituary at Darryl's funeral. Bill also wrote an article about Darryl for the Western Witness, the monthly publication of Western Bible Institute.[8] Distributed to a large constituency, Darryl's story generated a huge response as many people wrote

---

[8]   For the text of Bill Boyd's Western Witness article, see Appendix III

and requested multiple copies to share with friends. The impact of Bill's article in the Western Witness touched many lives.

Apparently, Bill continued to use Darryl as an example as he counseled students at Western in succeeding days. Years later, as Harvey and I served as representatives of Africa Inland Mission, we randomly stopped at a small Baptist Church in Cannon Beach, Oregon, on an Easter Sunday morning. With rain pouring down, we parked our vehicle and ran for cover into the foyer of the little church. Standing near the entrance, the pastor greeted us warmly. He asked our names since he had not seen us in his church before.

"You say you're Harvey Stranske?" Excitedly, he continued, "Did you have a son named Darryl, and did you teach at Western Bible Institute?"

Somewhat taken aback, Harvey replied, "Why, yes. How did you know?"

Almost unable to contain himself, our new friend responded that he attended Western soon after Harvey stopped teaching there. Bill Boyd noticed him faltering, called him in, and challenged him to persevere in his study and preparation for the ministry. As they talked, Bill told him Darryl's story and his unusual response to adversity, particularly in his life and death struggle with cancer. With tears in his eyes, he went on to say that God touched his life that day as Bill shared what it means to fully yield one's life to God's sovereign will. He left Bill's office a changed person, and indicated that the challenge of Darryl's life persuaded him to continue his preparation to become a minister.

We thanked God for giving us the privilege of catching another glimpse of His eternal purpose through our painful loss. It reminded us of the verse referring to Abel, "He being dead yet speaketh" (Hebrews 11:4).

A few years later our daughter-in-law gave us a copy of a sermon her brother had preached, including this excerpt:

> . . . I had an encounter which profoundly affected my life. My
> family was in Denver, Colorado, and we were going over to meet
> the family of my oldest sister's fiancé. We all piled into an old

Volkswagen Squareback and drove across town from where we were staying and tumbled out onto their front lawn with great excitement. We had a delicious dinner and then, as might be expected, the older kids gathered together and began laughing and joking, as did my parents. I found myself in a discussion with Darryl Stranske. Darryl was the brother of my now brother-in-law, Tim. He was 14, I was 12. What I especially remember about Darryl was his maturity. After only a few minutes speaking with him, it was apparent that this 14 year old, did not think like most 14 year olds. He did not act like them. He was different. In retrospect, I suppose that this was a very good thing because, you see Darryl was sick. He had leukemia . . . .

When I met Darryl, his leukemia was in remission . . . . Darryl explained how he had encountered many opportunities to explain why facing possible death did not hold any fear for him. Darryl was a believer in Jesus Christ and had no fear of Christ taking him home. As we talked I marveled, and I still do today, at the matter-of-fact way that Darryl explained his leukemia and the outlook for his life. His passion, he told me, was Jesus Christ. In the course of our conversation, he made a statement which I remember today . . . as if it were spoken yesterday. He told me, "John, if God can use my life more by taking me home than by leaving me here on earth, then that is what I want." Darryl Stranske's passion, at the age of 14, was that whatever should happen to his life, God would be glorified.

Darryl's leukemia eventually returned. It was [less than] two years later that I was awakened by my mother early one morning explaining that God had taken Darryl home to be with him. I sat for a few moments in the quiet of the early morning and recalled the one encounter I had with Darryl. In the midst of a great trial, of great difficulty, at an age when one should not have to contemplate death, Darryl met that trial with one desire that God should be glorified in it, and He was. He was.

Chapter 18

ONGOING STRUGGLES PROVIDE LESSONS IN GOD'S SOVEREIGNTY

I wish my feelings revealed the triumph expressed in many of the letters we received after Darryl's death but I have to admit, I struggled. Beyond losing Darryl, my whole world had changed. For more than a year and a half, doctor's appointments and meeting Darryl's needs day and night consumed me. Now Darryl was gone. The continuing shock almost overwhelmed me. I couldn't even pray for Darryl anymore; how I missed being able to talk to my Heavenly Father about him. I also missed interacting with my friends—doctors, personnel, and other parents—at the oncology clinic. My multiple losses and the sudden termination of life as I knew it left me with a gaping emptiness—a lonely feeling impossible to express in words.

After we returned from our recent trip to California, I wrote to my brother Wilbur and his wife sharing the deep, yet honest, feelings of my heart:

> On the way home Darryl just seemed to wilt. It's so funny how that medicine seemed to be working and then . . . reversed itself. These have . . . been hard weeks since we got back. But in spite of the trial of Darryl's illness, it is sweet to know the peace of God which passeth all understanding. We can trust in God who will do what is right in our lives and in Darryl's . . . .

I believed the truth of what I wrote. Knowing that God always does what is right and good in our lives provided peace beyond human understanding. Yet overpowering anguish gripped me, particularly as I thought back to the verses that had ministered to me early in Darryl's illness. On that night when I asked God if I should pray for Darryl's healing, I felt released to ask for this.

So now, I found myself in a struggle with God. Had God played games with me? That led me to think again of our tiny baby that died in Africa. And I cried out, "God, you already took one of our children. Why don't you pick on somebody else?"

I could not hear an answer. The heavens seemed as brass. Did God hear me? Did God care? Oh! I felt so alone! Job's desperate outcry reflected my feelings precisely, "I cry out to you O God, but you do not answer; I stand up, but you merely look at me" (Job 30:20 NIV).

I battled over this for months, but other issues also added to my unrest and that of our family. Darryl's long illness and death traumatized each of us in various ways. I later learned that others experience similar reactions. But at the time, those pressures added to my personal sense of inadequacy.

These circumstances also affected Harvey's and my personal relationship. Harvey, too, hurt and wanted my love and comfort during the grieving process. I had nothing left to give. When I lost my son, I lost part of me. My body felt dead, and this made it tough to respond to Harvey with the love and affection he craved.

My actions also affected the rest of the family. At one point, someone provided their rugged Rocky Mountain cabin for a short get-away. We drove to the cabin, anticipating healing as our family enjoyed hiking and the last of the summer beauty together. Sadness overcame me. Remembering how Darryl delighted in these mountains and his sheer enjoyment of God's handiwork rolled over me like a flood.

These memories pushed me over the brink; my emotions spun out of control. I broke out in tears, unable to think rationally. I had to leave—

immediately. I had to get back home! So we returned to Lakewood. This, of course, added to the growing alienation within our family. It upset Faith and Susan to leave so abruptly. They could not comprehend my actions. Actually, I couldn't understand them either.

Soon after we returned home, our seven-year old, Susan, found me in tears in my bedroom. Looking me in the face, she verbalized her feelings, "I bet you wish that you had never had Darryl. If you had never had him, then you wouldn't feel so bad."

"No, Susan, I don't wish that at all. It is just like if anything ever happened to you, I would never wish that you had never been. I would always want to remember what a joy you had been to us." My response satisfied her, even helping her to understand my deep feelings just a little.

Another time Susan shocked me by saying, "You know, when Darryl died Faith and I were glad to get rid of him, because we thought that you loved him and not us."

Her matter-of-fact statement stunned but informed me about those feelings. It opened the door for me to explain how much I loved her and Faith, even though Darryl's grave illness had required that I spend a great deal of time with him. Her comment also awakened me to my responsibility to refocus from my own grief to the needs of my precious girls and to recognize all that they, too, had encountered.

The expressed feelings of Susan and Faith reflected a response, often irrational, of many children in similar circumstances. In an article entitled, "Children Need Help Accepting Loved One's Death", Jane Estes, Staff Writer for the Star-News,[9] wrote,

> Mary Chess (8 years old) had seen her brother Chris for the
> first time since his brain tumor operation. She was riding home
> from the hospital with mother Carol when she cried, "I hope he
> dies. I don't get any attention anymore."

---

[9]   This article appears in a brochure, *Candlelighters of Pasadena*, reprinted from
the Star-News, Sunday, February 21, 1982.

> Shortly before Chris died several months later she went into his bedroom at home, shook him and cried, "Chris, wake up! You can't die!"
>
> Two weeks after he died, she was in the car with her mother when she cried, "I miss Chris so much. I don't have anybody to play with, and I don't have anybody to fight with."

These outbursts came from anger, fear and grief—all normal reactions for a child to the death of a loved one.

Some years later, I made the decision to return to school to take some English and writing courses. In a research paper, entitled, *The Effect of the Terminal Illness and Death of a Child on His Siblings*,[10] I wrote about families that had suffered experiences similar to ours. Plodding through many books and articles, I found that my feelings, the reactions of Darryl's siblings and the effects on our whole family reflected responses many suffer in comparable circumstances.

Often, children experiencing the trauma of losing a sibling become delinquents. Also, one authority stated that an astounding 70 percent of couples losing a child following a long illness separate or divorce. The husband desires his wife's physical love while the wife prefers no sexual intimacy. To preserve their marriage and keep their love alive, both must recognize each other's stress and accept their differing responses to it. Especially in the area of sexual intimacy, the husband must demonstrate restraint and consideration toward his aching wife and she, in turn, must stretch beyond her feelings or desires and give him the physical comfort and love for which he longs. Unresolved problems between the mother and father will, of course, spill over and affect their children.

As I continued my study, further healing occurred. Seeing that my feelings paralleled others in like circumstances brought relief. I discovered that Harvey and I reacted "normally" and in line with the responses of others who have experienced similar heartache and loss. However, healing is a slow

---

[10] The full text of my paper is printed in Appendix IV

process. Although a great amount of time had passed since Darryl stepped across that line into his heavenly home, and God made His peace real in my life, I continued to demean myself. I felt I had not stood as tall as I should.

Professional medical workers, social workers, psychologists and others working with terminally ill children wrote about all kinds of adverse effects experienced, not only during a long illness but, in a special way, when an illness ended in death. Common reactions include fear of going to bed, persistent and recurring nightmares or reverting to bed-wetting. What I discovered in my study corroborated the responses demonstrated within our family.

In hindsight, I realized I needed to take definitive action to comfort and help our girls during Darryl's long illness. They suffered emotional trauma and I failed to recognize it. Being caught up in my own struggles, along with trying to meet Darryl's needs, blinded me to the pressures on Faith and Susan. Had I seen beyond my own hurt, I would have worked harder to meet their needs during that difficult time.

While I maintained an evening reading time with Faith and Susan throughout Darryl's illness, they remembered little of this. I gave them my physical presence but I didn't connect with them emotionally. Writing the paper helped me understand the gulf that had grown between us.

Thinking through these matters I recognized a deeper conflict that had raged within me—a struggle that affected my relationship with God and, consequently, with my family members. I remembered the questions that had flooded my thoughts after Darryl's death. Where was God? Had He stopped caring for me? Was God fair to me? I now know that these feelings—these questions—often overcome people in similar circumstances.

We received a letter from New Jersey a few months after Darryl's death. It came from someone unknown to us who had friends who also encountered deep waters. The writer stated:

A few days ago I read the story of the death of your son Darryl in the Western Witness . . . . At 4:45 yesterday a fifteen-year-old boy, son of very dear friends of ours, died of cancer . . . .

The boy (an only child), Ronald, entered the hospital on July 4 of this year and about four or five weeks later the diagnosis was terminal cancer in the right axilla. This spread to the lungs. Suffering was intense and the boy refused morphine as long as possible as he wanted a clear mind for witnessing.

Ronald was an unusual boy, very mature both physically and spiritually for his years. His parents M. L. and R. are devoted to each other and the Lord. The three of them were a very close knit family and lived for each other. They were inclined to find no need for anyone else. Ronald had few friends of his own age, but preferred going everywhere and doing everything with his parents. During these four months of illness they all learned that they do need others and opened their hearts to others even as others opened their hearts to them.

Through his illness Ron had a glowing testimony. He witnessed for the Lord to doctors, nurses and patients. He had given his life to the Lord for full time ministry. We saw him change in those four months from a rather introverted boy to one who gave himself completely to others. He testified as did your son, that he could "thank God even for the cancer," because it was His will for him that day.

At the beginning his parents prayed that the Lord would either heal him or take him. They were willing for the Lord to take him. M.L. and R. clung to the Lord and the Word through months of suffering. They did not seek Scripture verses wildly, but in their regular daily study the Lord "gave" them verse upon verse and they became unshakably convinced that God was going to heal their boy and raise him up to serve Him. Prayer cells in many parts of the country brought this boy to the throne of grace . . . .

The Lord hasn't answered prayer as they anticipated. The weeks of extreme suffering seem unexplainable. We are several hundred miles from them and it is hard to judge reactions from this distance. Relatives said when they phoned last evening that the father is quite bitter. (He had asked us to pray that he would not become bitter, so he recognized this tendency). M.L. made the statement that the Lord had mocked her.

They have a real love for the Lord and the Word and a real devotional life. They have often said they would go into full-time-ministry if the Lord led. Now R. feels he can never stand before his adult S.S. [Sunday School] class and teach what he taught before. We are concerned that they will once more shut themselves off from others and not fulfill their ministry.

As you have been comforted and sustained by the Lord in your time of sorrow I thought you might have a word that will be of help to this couple.

Kay J.

Because of my continuing struggle and doubts at the time, I don't think I ever answered that letter. Interestingly, Harvey never struggled in the same way. However, receiving this letter provided added evidence that others reacted as I did. In fact, to deal with natural responses such as this, Dr. James Dobson wrote his helpful book, *When God Doesn't Make Sense*.

Continuing to ponder these matters, I reached several conclusions. Christians desperate to understand God's work in their lives during agonizing times, search for answers in their source book, God's Word. As they read—searching, pondering God's message to them—they find sustenance and strength. However, in our finite minds, potential danger lurks for those who desire God's Word to indicate the message they long to hear. Sometimes that urgent desire for a specific result moves one to grasp a particular promise in a way that differs from God's ultimate sovereignty and plan.

While I strove to surrender to God's will in Darryl's life, I believed He would glorify Himself through Darryl's healing. God is big enough to heal.

Jesus healed many people; his disciples healed people. God continues to heal people today. In fact, God's Word specifically tells us to pray for healing. "Is any one of you sick? He should call the elders of the church to pray over him . . . . And the prayer offered in faith will make the sick person well . . ." (James 5:14-15 NIV).

But God's Word also makes it clear that when we pray we must ask in keeping with God's will. ". . . [If] we ask anything according to his will, he hears us" (1 John 5:14). Even our Lord Jesus, pouring out His heart to His Father prior to His crucifixion, prayed, "My Father, if it is possible, may this cup be taken from me." But then added, "Yet not as I will, but as you will" (Matthew 26:39 NIV).

As we study God's Word we find issues and purposes beyond our human understanding that God causes or allows to happen. The Bible doesn't reveal this, but do you suppose that Eve ever understood why her son, Cain, murdered her righteous son, Able? Only as we come to the "faith chapter," do we catch a glimpse of at least one aspect of what God did through the death of Able, ". . . he was commended as a righteous man, when God spoke well of his offerings. And by faith he still speaks, even though he is dead" (Hebrews 11:4 NIV).

God made us with hearts and emotions that, in obedience to His plan, cause us to cleave to one another. This happens, in a special way, between a mother and her child. God has given parents the responsibility of protecting and shielding their child from harm and death. It is not unnatural, therefore, to plead with God to spare that precious life from death.

Our limited human vision often clouds our comprehension of God's ultimate purpose. We see what we think God could do by healing someone willing to live and witness for Him. God sees the higher, eternal purpose of His children and their circumstances bringing glory to His name. We fail to see the events that engulf us from God's perspective. But, God uses times of deep testing to give us increased perception of His greater purposes in our lives.

Through the deep waters of losing my beloved son, God began to give a new understanding of who He is, along with increasing ability to rest in the assurance that what He allows in my life is always best for me. I moved beyond my anguish and gave God thanks for accomplishing His purpose and for gaining glory through Darryl's life—and death.

While I never fully understood why God seemed to direct me to Psalm 41:2, "The Lord will preserve him and keep him alive . . . ," God used those words, and words which follow, to sustain and encourage me through the many difficult months of Darryl's illness. Certainly, those words helped me in making the right decision concerning psychological hypnosis for Darryl. God did "strengthen him upon the bed of languishing" (vs. 3) through those last days of his life, amazing his doctors as he never complained of pain. And God glorified His name as Darryl's doctors observed his response—a response that soared beyond their human comprehension.

Even before that, God had restored Darryl from his bed of sickness for a number of months—good months, in which God used Darryl's spoken word as well as his life. Contemplating these matters, God ministered to me, restoring peace and joy. He brought me to the place where, although a certain deep void occasionally rears its head in my life, I rest in the knowledge that He did everything right and good just as His Word promises. He answered prayer. He sustained Darryl meeting his needs and ours. He taught us many valuable lessons in the challenging days through which He led us. He worked in countless lives of others with whom we connected because of Darryl's illness.

God's Word reminds us, "For now we see through a glass, darkly; but then face to face: now I know in part; but then shall I know even as also I am fully known" (I Corinthians 13:12). In the end, when we stand complete in the presence of our eternal God, some things we valued on earth will lose their luster. Our perspective will change when viewed in the light of our eternal home.

When I read many of the things that Darryl wrote and remember what he said, I know that God answered the desire of his heart. The latter years of his life became a living example of daily walking close to his Lord and Master. He lived life to the full and enjoyed each day even in his debilitating illness. Yet he looked forward, with constant longing, to being with Jesus. To Darryl, Philippians 1:21, "For to me to live is Christ, and to die is gain," became a daily reality. This reflected a conscious walk with his Lord requiring only one further step to enter into the immediate presence of the Savior whom he served. We observed him begin to take this final step toward heaven as he spoke his last words, "That's the place where Jesus . . . That's the place where He . . ." He followed up those faltering sentences with, "Jesus died for your sins and for my sins. I'm going to see Him." We believe these words inscribed on his tombstone in the cemetery where we placed his body in Golden, Colorado, give a further testimony of God's grace to some who pause to read it.

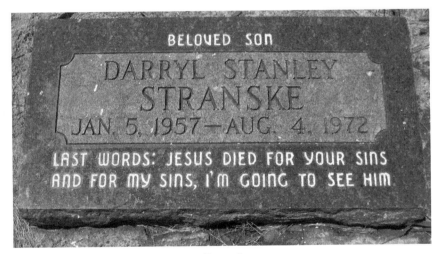

Darryl's tombstone

We will never know all that God has and will accomplish in the hearts of people because of Darryl's story, but we thank God that He allowed us to see a small part of what He has done.

As I think back to our family gathering—nineteen months before Darryl's death—I can't help but notice the correlation between that beautiful Christmas tree candle melting down to reveal the beauty inside and Darryl's life melting away to display the incredible beauty of a life under God's control. Darryl accomplished his great desire to magnify Christ in his life and in his death. To God be the glory!

Appendix I

HOW DO I MAKE LIFE'S MOST IMPORTANT DECISION TO BECOME A CHRISTIAN?

(Scripture quotations are NIV)

First, you must recognize that you are a sinner (we all are!). Romans 3:23 (NIV) says, "For ALL have sinned and fall short of the glory of God." As much as we might want to, we can't reach God's perfect standard on our own. Even if I'm a "pretty good" person . . . I go to church; I even pray; I give money to the poor; I don't lie or cheat or steal; and I'm overall a kind and thoughtful person . . . God says these "best" things about me are like filthy rags to Him! (Isaiah 64:6) And, "the wages of sin is DEATH." Romans 6:23 (NIV) Still, God loves us so much! In Romans 5:8 (NIV) He says, "But God demonstrates His love toward us in this, while we were still sinners, Christ died for us." You see, since I'm a sinner and I could not achieve God's perfect holiness on my own, I needed a savior. I needed a perfect sacrifice. Some people try to find that savior in other gods. They hope they'll find their god's acceptance somehow. But God says, "Neither is there salvation in any other for there is no other name [Jesus] under heaven given among men whereby we must be saved." Acts 4:12 (NIV) Jesus also said, "I am the way, the truth, and the life. No man comes to the Father except through me." John 14:6 (NIV) The foundational message in the Bible is found in I Corinthians

15:3,4 (NIV) ". . . that Christ died for our sins according to the Scriptures, that he was buried, that he was raised on the third day according to the Scriptures". According to Romans 10:9 (NIV), ". . . if you confess with your mouth 'Jesus is Lord' and believe in your heart that God raised him from the dead, you will be saved." Saved from what? According to Matthew 25:41, those who do not belong to Him, He will tell to depart from him into the eternal fire prepared for the devil and his angels. God certainly doesn't want this! He says in 2 Peter 3:9 that His desire is for all to come to repentance. He won't barge his way in though. He gives each of us a choice. Are you ready to receive His forgiveness and bask in the love of your Heavenly Father? He waits with open arms to receive YOU into His family! All you need to do is talk to Him. Pray a prayer like this:

> *Dear Heavenly Father,*
> *I admit that I am a sinner in need of a savior. There's nothing I can do on my own to receive your favor. I believe that Jesus died in my place to pay the penalty for my sin and that you rose again. I surrender my life to you and trust you as my Savior and Lord. Thank you for forgiving me. Help me to grow in you and live a life that pleases you.*
> *In Jesus' Name, Amen.*

If you have surrendered your heart to Jesus, you will meet Darryl one day! And even more important, you will also see Jesus face to face and "dwell in the house of the Lord forever!" Psalm 23:6 (NIV)

Appendix II

ROCKY MOUNTAIN NEWS ARTICLE, JANUARY 24, 1971

The Sunday edition, January 24, 1971, of the Rocky Mountain News featured the following article about Darryl on its front page. Accompanied by a 5 x 8 inch picture of Darryl holding his violin, the Saturday night edition carried a title line, "He's not afraid to die." Replacing that statement the Sunday morning edition caption said, "I want Christ to be magnified . . ." The article, in its entirety, follows:

* * *

Lakewood youth, 14, maintains faith, courage 'in the valley of shadow of death'

By ALAN CUNNINGHAM
Rocky Mountain News Writer

Darryl Stranske has lost a little weight, and he laughs when you point out that he has the "jail-house pallor" one acquires from spending a month or more in hospital beds.

It wouldn't be hard to believe that the 14-year old Lakewood youngster's recent surgery had solved the problems which have plagued him for much of the last two years. And it would have been a simple matter for this family to leave such people as the neighbors and his teachers at Dunstan Junior High School with that impression.

Wanted people to know why

But the Stranske family doesn't believe in doing things that way. They wanted people to know exactly why it was that Darryl hadn't been carrying his newspaper route lately—and why he probably wouldn't get to carry it again.

So it was that the week before last Mr. and Mrs. Stranske asked the new carrier on Darryl's former route, William "Butch" Hrouda, to distribute copies of a mimeographed letter along with that morning's papers.

"Dear Neighbor," it began. "Our son, Darryl, has been your Rocky Mountain News boy during the past few months. We have just been told that Darryl has a highly malignant type of cancer. The doctors feel that there is no medicine which can cure this and that Darryl has only a short time to live."

The message must have shocked many of the more than 100 families who saw it. But it didn't end with this blunt statement.

Entire, remarkable story

It went on, in fact to explain the entire story of a young man with the courage and faith to remain at peace—even to keep his sense of humor going—as he looks death in the eye.

On a day when the smog doesn't interfere, people in the Green Mountain area of Lakewood can look out over a marvelous view of the downtown skyline. At night, they can see the city lights as they stretch for miles, and even the landing lights of jets as they touch down at Stapleton International Airport 15 miles away.

When you seat yourself in their spacious and pleasantly furnished living room at 12284 W. Tennessee Ave., talking to Darryl, his parents and brothers and sisters, it is impossible to find any sense of gloom, even as they all talk about the hard facts of what is going on in Darryl's life.

Darryl was born in Turlock, Calif. on Jan. 5, 1957, while his parents were on home leave from a tour of duty as missionaries for the non-denominational Africa Inland Mission in Sudan.

They went back to Africa for another four and one-half years after that, then spent an equal period in Turlock once again before Stranske came to Lakewood in 1966 to teach at the Western Bible Institute in Morrison.

As the fourth oldest of six children (three boys and three girls), Darryl quickly developed into a wholesome, ambitious and bright youngster with as many interests as a boy could be expected to have. He learned to play the violin and the piano, enjoyed swimming and bike riding, yet at the same time was an A student in school.

Last year, when he was in the seventh grade, Darryl made the honor roll with A's in every subject but one, where he got a B. He did almost as well this fall, in spite of the fact that he started missing school frequently at Thanksgiving time because a gland on the left side of his jaw was swelling up so badly that it pinched some nerves.

In the fall of 1969, Darryl asked Rocky Mountain News distributor James K. Harvey for a paper route in his area. Harvey said the nearest one was a mile from his home, but Darryl took it on and won the admiration of his customers there. Before he switched to a route closer to home last August, one customer who was leaving town gave him a frisky miniature poodle named Snowball.

And somewhere in the midst of all his other activities, the busy teen-ager took charge of the care and feeding of an aquarium full of fish in the family dining room.

Several years ago

Darryl's glands started giving him trouble a couple of years ago, and doctors now think that may be when the malignant cells started multiplying in his body.

It was only last summer, however when Darryl had a minor collision with the safety bar of a roller coaster at a local amusement park—then suffered intense pains in his jaw that night—that anyone realized something serious might be the matter. In early December, the swelling was so great that he went into Swedish Hospital for tests.

Later he was transferred to Porter Memorial hospital, where surgeons removed the gland. There was hope at the time that this might solve Darryl's problem—except that the doctors found indications of malignancy in the surrounding lymph nodes. They performed a biopsy, and the report came back positive.

"We hadn't told Darryl," his father explained, "but we were pretty sure of the implications since after Christmas. The doctors told us that, because of the rapid spread of the disease through his lymph glands, they knew what it had to be."

It was on Monday Jan. 11, a Monday night only six days after Darryl had celebrated his birthday in a hospital bed (and had been unable to eat any of his own cake due to impending surgery) that the biopsy results confirmed those fears. Physicians said Darryl would have to begin undergoing weekly treatments at the Children's Hospital oncology clinic, and said he might as well be told the whole truth.

Stranske visited his son that night in the hospital. He began their conversation by reading Darryl a couple of passages from the New Testament chapter called Philippians, which sets forth a letter that the apostle Paul wrote from a jail cell to those in the church at Philippi.

As a prisoner of the Romans Paul knew his life was in jeopardy. But his letter showed he was prepared to accept any fight so long as it served "to magnify Christ," and to help spread the message followers of Jesus had vowed to send forth as widely as they could.

"But I would ye should understand, brethren, that the things which happened to me have fallen out rather unto the furtherance of the gospel."

Paul wrote, ". . . and many of the brethren in the Lord, waxing confident by my bonds, are much more bold to speak the word without fear . . ."

"According to my earnest expectation and my hope, that in nothing I shall be ashamed but that with all boldness as always, so now also Christ shall be magnified in my body, whether it be by life, or by death."

'To live is Christ'

"For me to live is Christ, and to die is gain."

After reading these and other verses, Stranske told Darryl about the medical report. Then he asked his son what his reaction was. The boy replied that his feelings were best described as being similar to those expressed by Paul in his letter to Philippi.

"I told Dad that, whatever it is, if God's got his hand in it, it is actually for the best," Darryl explained this week. "Jesus Christ said everybody should be a witness, and I said that, through this, I had a better opportunity to tell people about my Lord Jesus Christ."

They talked some more, then Darryl asked his father to read one more Biblical quotation, the 23rd psalm (sic).

In the letter which went out to subscribers on Darryl's paper route, his father quoted his boy's comment after that:

"Just think, Dad, I'm walking in the valley of the shadow of death. And Dad, I'm not afraid because God IS with me!"

This week Darryl's parents explained that the only time his father had ever had to help him on the paper route before he got sick was on Sundays, when they hurried through the deliveries together in order to get to Sunday School and worship services at the Judson Memorial Baptist Church in Denver. Darryl said he had "known Christ as my Savior since I was real young."

Lately, however, he says his faith has deepened and he has spent more time with his Bible or in prayer.

His mother, Mrs. Evadene Stranske, said the circumstances "also have made us aware how temporary life is on earth—and how flat all the houses and cars and all the business about a 'better everything' and not only keeping up with the Joneses but having something better that the Joneses really is."

Such feelings compelled Darryl's parents to try and share their current crisis—and their belief that it has brought them closer to reality than most of us come in our daily lives—with everyone on their son's paper route. Apparently, many who read it agreed.

'Sort of amazing'

"The response has been sort of amazing," his father said. "Our telephone was just ringing constantly for the first couple of days. We found there were a number of people who knew what we were talking about in the letter in relation to Jesus Christ."

Others, said his wife, "wondered how we could have peace and Darryl could have peace in the face of something like this. This is what they wanted to know."

Darryl's own sense of peace is reflected by the matter-of-fact way in which he answers questions about his condition. He is as familiar as his parents with the medical terms the family has learned from nine doctors who have been drawn into the case over the last couple of months.

He doesn't know exactly how much more time he has to live because the doctors don't either. They classify his condition as lymphosarcoma, but haven't pinned it down to one explicit type of cancer. A virus-related strain, isolated by a physician in Africa, could be present.

He'll have to undergo periodic treatment at Children's including a highly painful removal of bone marrow samples every three months, which has led Darryl to say jokingly that he's not sure it is worth living through the procedure very many times.

The Stranskes letter included a postscript which noted that God and medical science might be able to collaborate on a miracle to save Darryl's life, and asked for prayers "that God's perfect will might be done in Darryl's body."

Should it be God's will for Darryl to live, he believes he would devote his life to a religious calling. But both he and his parents share the conviction that was stated in the postscript:

"We do not ask for this unless God can be glorified through it. We agree with Darryl that we want Christ to 'be magnified . . . . whether it be by life or by death.'"

Appendix III

WESTERN WITNESS ARTICLE, SEPTEMBER, 1972

The *Western Witness*, Bulletin of the Western Bible Institute, for September, 1972, featured an article, "Darryl Stranske, Beneath the Cross," by Bill Boyd. The front of the *Western Witness* carried a copy of the Rocky Mountain News photo by Mel Schieltz, a smiling Darryl holding his violin. The entire text of that article follows:

* * *

What kind of men comprise the faculty of Western Bible Institute? The acid test, of course, is what kind of fruit they produce. As a school we can say the men on the faculty are able to infect the students with the quality of life that manifests the indwelling Christ. But do they? Or is it purely an academic exercise differing from secular institutions only in that the students memorize the Kings of Israel instead of algebraic equations?

There are few situations in life where we are as "real" as we are in our homes; and there are few tests that better calibrate the spiritual life of the home than the lives of its children.

Having prepared the "test situation" and, in a sense, placed our faculty members on the scales, let me share with you the recent obituary given at the funeral of Darryl Stranske, the son of one of our faculty members, Harvey Stranske.

15 year old Darryl Stranske of 12284 West Tennessee Avenue died Friday morning, the 4th of August, of cancer of the lymph glands that had turned to leukemia. He attended Dunstan Jr. High School, managing not only to keep up his 9th grade work during his illness, but to even achieve straight A's during his last semester.

Darryl was a paper boy for Rocky Mountain News, the paper that did a front page story on his life and illness in January of 1971. Grace Calvary Church is the church where Darryl was a member.

He is survived by his mother and father, Mr. and Mrs. Harvey Stranske, 2 brothers, Ray and Tim, and 3 sisters, Charlotte, Faith and Susie.

He is also survived by 3 grandparents, Mr. and Mrs. Ephraim Stranske and Mrs. Lillian Johnson, and by a number of aunts, uncles and cousins.

Most obituaries would end here—but Darryl was different, as all who knew him would testify, for Darryl is survived by some other relatives.

He is survived by another brother, a Jr. High classmate who through Darryl's testimony knelt in Darryl's living room to invite Jesus Christ to become the Savior and Lord of his life—and thereby became a brother in Christ to Darryl.

He is survived by a number of brothers and sisters he has never yet met. One Sunday morning in January, 1971, just after doctors diagnosed Darryl's illness, The Rocky Mountain News took its entire front page of the Sunday paper to share Darryl's story. The essence of his testimony that they printed was Darryl's desire to see the outworking of some Scripture verses, Philippians 1:20-21, manifested in his life.

That Christ shall even now as always be exalted in my body, whether by life or by death: For to me to live is Christ, to die is gain.

That Sunday morning the story of Darryl Stranske was the source of many of the Sunday morning sermons here in Denver as well as other pulpits in this country. One teenager from a church on the north side of Denver called and said, "We haven't had anybody saved in our church in several years. But this morning when the pastor preached about Darryl, there were 14 people saved." So Darryl is survived by 14 brothers and sisters he has never met.

Only God knows how many brothers and sisters there are like that, for many people have used his story to illustrate the life of faith and God seems to bless it in an unusual way. His aunt recently shared his life story with some children and they all seemed to be supernaturally moved; in fact 4 received Christ.

Darryl is also survived by an innumerable host of people that took comfort and drew strength from his life of faith. He received letters from people in 23 states, the District of Columbia, 3 foreign countries, and also a personal letter from the President of the United States, Richard Nixon. I'd like to share a few of the survivors of that innumerable host and how they were blessed.

First, there was Aunt Helen. Aunt Helen is a semi-invalid who has been afflicted with a bone disease most of her life and lives here in Denver. She isn't really an 'aunt' but Darryl grew to know her and called her 'aunt.' They would talk from time to time and share what God was doing in their lives. To her Darryl's life of faith was a constant encouragement. She said, "When I became discouraged with my burden of illness, I would just pick up Darryl's story (which is always kept beside her) and read it again. And I'd take courage. Here is one letter Darryl wrote to Aunt Helen:

> Dear Aunt Helen,
> Thought I'd send a little something to cheer ya'. We have some irises on the dining room table, so I decided to draw one. When I got finished I thought it might be something you might like, so I sent it to you.
> Isn't it neat to know that pretty soon we get to see Jesus, who is more glorious than the prettiest iris?!
>
> Love in Christ,
> Darryl

Another group were people who came to his room. Darryl was always ready—not to take sympathy—but to share the unsearchable riches of his living Christ. Let me illustrate: toward the last, one of the doctors informed him they were taking him off of his medicine because his body was rejecting it, and it was only adding pain and causing problems for him. This was Darryl's response to the last human hope of life.

He said to his father, "Dad, print a verse for me and make it large enough so everyone can see it when they come into the room."

The verse?—"Yea, though I walk thru the valley of the shadow of death, I will fear no evil."

The doctors who treated that body of clay were not unmoved by this young man's life. Some of the doctors who were on Darryl's case during most of its duration spoke of the difference of his life.

Shortly after Darryl's death one doctor said, "We've sort of felt during the last month or two, that even though we were the ones that were supposed to be taking care of Darryl, he was really the one taking care of us." They could analyze the illness in his body—but they were mystified by the person that dwelt within. They realized Darryl was different than most people on the operating table, that he was different from themselves, and that that difference was not the body—but the difference was the person of Jesus Christ who lived within Darryl.

Darryl's own Dad was influenced by his son's life. About three weeks before his homegoing, while hospitalized and in particular pain, almost involuntarily, as would be so natural, his father said, "Poor, Darryl." Smiling his winsome smile in spite of the pain, Darryl looked up and said, "Dad, I'm not poor! Since this is what my Heavenly Father has planned for me just now, this is the very best thing that could be happening to me. So don't call me poor!"

At this point, most of us are tempted to say, "What an incredible person!" But Darryl would respond to me and to you as he did to the people who said it, "No, I'm not incredible but I have someone living inside me who is—the Lord Jesus."

Darryl closes this obituary by sharing with you and me how the Lord Jesus taught him to cope with pain: when it seemed to be unbearable, Darryl would think of His Savior dying on the cross in pain and suffering for him. Then he would reflect that "if the Lord Jesus could bear that for my sake, then I can surely bear the suffering that God has given to me—for Christ's sake."

If we could sum up Darryl's life we would have to say, he learned the secret of his favorite song—how to live Beneath the Cross of Jesus."

That's a thumb nail sketch of the life of Darryl—and by virtue of their relationship—a miniature portrait of Harvey. It might be interesting to know that at the cemetery when the pastor finished the brief ceremony, Harvey said, "Pastor, can we close by singing, To God Be the Glory?"

Thank you, Harvey, for your life and ministry in our midst—but to God be the glory.

Appendix IV

PAPER: THE EFFECTS OF A TERMINAL ILLNESS AND DEATH OF A CHILD ON HIS SIBLINGS

Growing out of observations and questions raised through Darryl's illness and death I wrote *The Effects of the Terminal Illness and Death of a Child on His Siblings* as a term paper in an English course which I took several years after Darryl died. Doing the research necessary to complete this paper helped me to appreciate that many feelings and reactions which members of our family experienced were often observed in others going through similar circumstances. The paper is reproduced here, in its entirety, including the bibliography which alludes to many other works which had been written to address these issues at that time.

* * *

The Effects of the Terminal Illness and Death
of a Child on His Siblings

During the terminal illness of a child, the siblings are usually the forgotten sufferers. "Justifiably they may feel, 'If you're the sick one everybody cares. If you're the brother or sister, they don't give a hoot.'"[1] This uncaring attitude is not intentional but is precipitated by the trauma that the ill child and the parents experience which overshadows the needs of the other children. In the last few years, professional medical workers, social workers, psychologists and others working with terminally ill children have begun to realize that this is an area that has been overlooked. The illness does not effect the ill child only but the psychological health and well being of the whole family. There is one set of problems that the well sibling faces during the illness while other pressures trouble the child after his brother or sister has died.

Children are first faced with perplexing problems at the onset of a terminal illness. The siblings are often neglected which is not perceived by the parents who are disoriented due to the anxiety through which they are going. One reason they are neglected is because the shocked parents center their attention on the ill child while the sibling receives little or no concern.[2] Parents are forced to be away at the hospital leaving children with relatives, friends, neighbors or to fend for themselves.[3] Also the parents naturally need to spend much time with the ailing child which forces them to become a unit. This excludes the sibling making him feel isolated from the family.[4] The mother's absence means that the house is not kept up, clothes unwashed, and meals are haphazard.[5] This generates a whole cycle of unhappiness as the pressures and tiredness cause the mother to become irritable. She then takes out her frustrations on the siblings.[6] Since the illness brings on heavy financial burdens, siblings do not get their clothing needs met and are not able to do the special things that they have done in the past.[7]

This is done by parents who want to shield their children and refuse to tell them what illness the child has and the possibility that it is terminal. Since the child usually figures this out anyway, holding back information is fruitless.[8] "The parents, siblings and certainly the terminally ill child, all need an atmosphere of support (openness) and encouragement, freeing them to express their fears and concerns. Such an environment is instrumental in alleviating death anxiety, as well as feelings of isolation and loneliness."[9] When siblings are not told about the disease, they tend to fantasize, wonder how it will affect them and whether or not they will die afflicted in the same manner.[10] Older children are especially concerned about "genetic implications" which should be explained if there are any."[11] In keeping the lines of communication open, children should be informed about lab and diagnostic test results, changes in diet, and the possibility of death's imminence.[12]

One disease about which it is exceedingly hard to be open is Cystic Fibrosis, a genetically based disease, because more than one child in a family is often afflicted. Creative ways of handling this situation should be explored.[13] Generally, in most types of illness, "age appropriate" communication helps the siblings to adapt to a period of neglect, and makes the child feel included which "minimizes jealousy" and "promotes cooperation."[14]

The children can be expected to show regressive behavior to which the parents should be alerted. The illness may affect the child's academic ability.[15] It is possible that the child would regress in his interaction with other children.[16] Misbehavior is a sign that a child is suffering, so parents and also teachers should be understanding at this time. A study done in Florida of the siblings of ill children showed that many "conformers displayed delinquent behavior" at the time of the terminal illness of a brother or sister.[17] With many children there will be "somatic distress (sighing, weakness, fatigue and gastronomical problems).[18] Children usually have guilt reactions thinking that they caused the illness.[19] Sibling rivalry may increase between the well and ill child which needs to be dealt with, but discipline should be modified in this area.[20]

Some children are at greater risk than others. The sibling whose mother has to be away in a distant city for long periods of time for the ill child's treatment, is disrupted from his bonding to his mother causing severe regression.[21] Children are more vulnerable when they have a single parent because child care and expense is not shared with another person.[22] Some families already have an ill member, and this increases the potential for disorientation with the children.[23] When the ill child is a twin, it is especially devastating for the twin brother or sister which was exemplified in the story of the Ipswitch twins.[24] The ill twin was very provoked with his brother, Steve, who kept going into his room during the night to see if he was all right. It is also very difficult for the child in the family that has experienced several deaths.[25] A sibling with poor parental relations or poor relations with the ill child can be expected to have trouble coping with the situation.[26] Within a family, the most vulnerable child is always the child closest in age to the ill sibling.[27]

When a child dies, there are special considerations to be noted. It is very important that mourning be experienced together. People often wonder about the wisdom of permitting children to attend the funeral. Most children under six are too young to attend, but it is considered beneficial for an older child.[28] In Zilig's book, a case study was done on a six and a half year old child who had deep psychological problems because he did not attend the funeral and had no idea what happened to his baby brother. After psychological therapy and understanding that his brother was buried, the child improved.[29] A child should be able to go to the funeral if he wants but should not be forced to go if there is fear and hesitation.[30] Attending the funeral helps the child to experience the loss in a concrete way.[31] A child who expresses his grief through physical exertion, should not be criticized since children do not react in the same way as an adult. A child who goes out and plays ball or becomes involved in active play should not be thought to be disrespectful or uncaring.[32]

The mourning period continues for many months beyond the funeral, and it is important that the parents be "models of grief.[33] On his tape, Bayly gives an example of a child who thought his parents did not care about his brother's death because he had never seen them cry.[34] Children should never be sent away at this time but should hear what is said and see their parent's tears.[35] "Children need to be treated as naturally as possible. Sharing feelings at this time and talking together about the death can gradually make the loss more bearable."[36] When trying to "heal the survivors," a creative idea is to ask the siblings about their memories of the dead child on his birthday.[37]

Children have many misunderstandings about death and need to be helped to a correct view. There is little real understanding among young children. Children between ages three and five, who think the dead person is sleeping and will awaken are reinforced by parents who speak of death as sleep.[38] Children from five to nine fear death and think death can catch you so you must be watching and thereby escape.[39] Since the ages from nine to twelve are a period of no special demands, there is less death anxiety than for the younger or older child.[40]

Children need to be helped to understand what death actually is. "Death education begins naturally the first time the young child sees a dead bird or plant; it continues when the child grieves for the death of loved ones . . . . [41] It should be explained that when a person dies, he does not move, or breathe, or think, or feel. Since television has given children unrealistic ideas about death, it is important to correct these misunderstandings.[42] This is a good time to stress religious beliefs, for example, by telling a child, "She is at home with Jesus."[43]

Following death the surviving child needs help in understanding and dealing with many other difficulties. The paramount problem is that the marriage of the parents may be in jeopardy. Elizabeth Kubler Ross says, "70% of parents after the loss of a child are in a period of separation or divorce afterward."[44] When the marriage fails the children experience the pain of being separated from one of their parents, in addition to the disruption of home life caused by the illness and death.

The regressive behaviors that were noted at the onset of the illness are now intensified with added problems. Upon seeing that a brother or sister could die, the sibling becomes fearful that his parents or he, himself, might die.[45] He may be afraid to go to bed, experience nightmares or begin bed wetting again. The child may interpret the "preoccupation" of the parental mourning as a repudiation of himself causing deep-seated feelings of inferiority.[47] Children may remember that they had told the one who had died, "I wish you were dead," making them fear that they actually caused the death.[48] The child who has died may be considered a rival when a parent compares the two, causing the living child to feel that his own death was preferred.[49] Problems which are not resolved in childhood have been known to cause emotional illness into adult life.[50]

After the death of the child, the family finds a new "identity." They no longer have an ill child, but one less family member. This gives them the mobility to do the things that they have not been able to do for some time. Once again they will be able to take trips and do other things that are considered special for the siblings. They will again have the time they need to spend with the other children and to meet their needs.[51]

In spite of the difficulties connected with the terminal illness and death of a sibling, there are some good effects brought about by the experience. Many parents and children discover that they were able to cope with something they would have thought impossible, and are rewarded by the realization that they are stronger people than they had thought.[52] Children learn to be brave and they learn that pain can be born.[53] Suffering has a "leveling" effect on a family as the children discern that their parents need them.[54] This helps the children to have an early understanding of their parents.[55] The illness can bring about a very special family closeness as stated by Noto concerning his sister, "During her illness, Tina brought our family closer than we had ever been.[56]

End Notes

1   Martha J. Craft, "The Suffering Child." The American Journal of Maternal Child Nursing, 5, Sept./Oct. (1979), p. 297. Taken from: Jo-Eileen Gyulay, The Dying Child (New York, McGraw-Hill Book Co.,1978) p. 41.

2   Joseph Bayly, The Suffering Child (Michigan City, Indiana, Sound Word, 1979) Tape 104, Side 2.

3   Holly Ann Williams, Frederick P. Rivara and Michael B. Rothenberg, "The Child is Dying: Who Helps the Family?" The American Journal of Maternal Child Nursing, 6, Nov./Dec. 1980, p. 12.

4   Sue Childers Taylor, R.N., MS., MEd., P.N.P. "Siblings Need a Plan of Care Too," Pediatric Nursing, 6, Nov./Dec. 1980, p. 12.

5   Elizabeth R. Pritchard et al. Home Care Living with Dying (New York, Columbia Univ. Press. 1979), p. 201.

6   Ibid.

7   Robert L. Noland, Counceling Parents of the Ill and Handicapped, (Springfield, Ill., Charles C. Thomas Publisher, 1971) p. 49.

8   Elaine Ipswitch, Scott Was Here (New York, Delacorte Press, 1979) p. 185.

9   Richard Lonetto PhD., Children's Conception of Death. (New York, Springer Publishing, 1980) p. 178.

10 Taylor, p. 12.

11 Ibid.

12 Craft, p. 299.

13 Prichard, p. 261.

14 Marjorie J. Smith et al., Child and Family (New York, McGraw-Hill, 1982) p.530.

15 Bernard Spilka, Georgia M. Zwartjes, and William J. Zwartjes M.D., "Students with Cancer." Today's Education, 70, No. 4 (1981) p. 23.

16 Ibid.

17 Bayly, Tape 104, side 1.

18 Craft, p. 299.

19 Williams, Rivara and Rothenberg, p. 262.

20 Craft, p. 300.

21 Jane Estes, "Children Need Help Accepting Loved One's Death," Star News. 21 Feb., 1982, p. 6.

22 Williams, Rivara and Rothenberg, p. 262.

23 Ibid.

24 Ipswitch, p. 56.

25 Williams, Rivara and Rothenberg, p. 262.

26 Taylor. p. 10.

27 Ibid., p. 12.

28 Noland, p. 516.

29 Rose Zeligs, Ed.D. Children's Experiences with Death. (Springfield, Ill., Charles C. Thomas Publisher, 1974) pp. 6-10.

30 Noland, p. 516.

31 Ibid.

32 Ibid., p. 515.

33 Bayly, Tape 104, side 2.

34 Ibid.

35 Christine L. Roberts, "Helping Children Cope with Death," Educational Leadership, 38, No. 5 (1981) p. 0-411.

36 A.J. Pope, "Children's Attitudes Toward Death," Health Education, 10, No. 3 (1979) p. 28.

37 Bayly, Tape 104, side 2.

38 Morris A. Wessel, "Coping with Death," Parents, June 1981, p. 34.

[39]   Lonetto, p. 165.

[40]   Ibid., p. 136.

[41]   Roberts, p. 411.

[42]   Pope, p. 29.

[43]   Ida Marie Martinson, Home Care for the Dying Child. Professional and Family Perspectives. (New York, Appleon Century Crafts, 1976) p. 11.

[44]   Bayly, Tape 104, side 2.

[45]   Smith, p. 531.

[46]   Rachael T. Hare-Mustin, "Family Therapy Following the Death of a Child," Journal of Marital and Family Therapy, 5, No. 2 (1979), p. 31.

[47]   Ibid.

[48]   Bayly, Tape 104, side 1.

[49]   Hare-Musstin, p. 31.

[50]   Zeligs, p. 114.

[51]   Martinson, p. 109.

[52]   Jerome L. Schulman, Coping with Tragedy. Successfully Facing the Problems of a Seriously Ill Child, (Chicago, Follet Publishing 1976) p. 323.

[53]   Bayly, Tape 104, Side 1.

[54]   Ibid.

[55]   Ibid.

[56]   Dante Noto, "I Remember Tina." Seventeen, Sept. 1979, p. 76.

Bibliography

Bayly. Joseph. The Suffering Child. Michigan City, Indiana: Sound Word, 1979. Tape 104.

Craft, Martha J. "Help for the Family's Neglected Other Child." The American Journal of Maternal Child Nursing, 5, Sept./Oct. 1979, pp. 297-300.

Cunningham, Alan. "A Lesson in Young Courage". Rocky Mountain News. August 1972, op-ed page.

Cunningham, Alan. "Lakewood youth maintains persistent courage, faith". Rocky Mountain News. 24 January 1971, p. 1

Estes, Jane. "Children Need Help Accepting Loved One's Death." Star News. 21 Feb. 1982, p. 6.

Hare-mustin, Rachael T. "Family Therapy Following the Death of a Child." Journal of Marital and Family Therapy, 5. No. 2 (1979), pp. 27-35.

Ipswitch, Elaine. Scott Was Here. New York: Delacorte Press, (1979.

Lonetto, Richard PhD. Children's Conception of Death. New York: Springer Publishing, 1980.

Martinson, Ida Marie. Home Care for the Dying Child. Professional and Family Perspectives. New York: Appleon Century Crofts, 1976.

Maxwell, L. E. Crowded to Christ. Grand Rapids, Michigan: Wm. B. Eerdmans Publishing Company, 1952.

Noland, Robert L. Counseling Parents of the Ill and Handicapped. Springfield, Ill.: Charles C. Thomas Publisher, 1971

Noto, Dante. "I Remember Tina." Seventeen, Sept. 1979, pp. 72-76.

Pope, A.J. "Children's Attitude Toward Death." Health Education, 10, No. 3 (1979), 27-29.

Prichard, Elizabeth R., et al. Home Care Living with Dying. New York: Columbia Univ. Press, 1979.

Roberts, Christine L. "Helping Children Cope with Death." Educational Leadership, 38, No. 5 (1981). pp. 409-411.

Schulman, Jerome L., M.D. Coping with Tragedy. Successfully Facing the Problem of a Seriously Ill Child. Chicago: Follet Publishing, 1976.

Smith, Marjorie J., et al. Child and Family. New York: McGraw Hill, 1982.

Spika, Bernard, Georgia M. Zwartjes and William J. Zwartjes, M.D. "Student with Cancer." Today's Education, 70, No. 4 (1981), pp. 18-23.

Taylor, Sue Childers, R.N., M.S. MEd., P.I.V.P. "Siblings Need a Plan of Care Too." Pediatric Nursing, 6, Nov./Dec. 1980, pp. 9-13.

Wessel, Morris A. "Coping with Death." Parents. Jan. 1981, p. 34.

Williams, Holly Ann, Fredrick P. Rivara, and Michael B. Rothenberg. "The Child is Dying: Who Helps the Family?" The American Journal of Maternal Child Nursing, 6, No. 4 (1981), pp. 261-265.

Zeligs, Rose, Ed.D. Children's Experience with Death. Springfield, Ill.: Charles C. Thomas Publisher, 1974.

About The Author

Evadene Stranske encountered one of life's most excruciating experiences—illness and death of a son. Because he lived an extraordinary testimony, she has desired to share it. In preparation, she returned to school as an English major and graduated with honors at age sixty-one. She hopes this book encourages you!